PMP® Exam Preparation

600 Questions with Explanations
based on the
PMBOK® Guide Fifth Edition

Daud Nasir, PMP

ISBN: 1-4923-8876-9
ISBN-13: 978-1-4923-8876-0

CONTENTS

1 INSTRUCTIONS

The following tips will enhance your learning experience and help boost your chances of success in the actual PMP® exam.

Take each of the tests as a whole by setting aside 4 hours. The actual test is 4 hours long. The time does not stop once it starts. However, you can take breaks, if you like, but the clock keeps ticking.

Have few blank sheets of paper and pencil ready before you start the test. You will receive the same when taking the actual test. This can be used for performing calculations, or taking notes to analyze choices.

You are to look for the best choice as the answer to each of the questions. This means there can be one or more choices that are valid and correct but may not be the best choice(s).

Target about 50 questions per hour if you continue to attempt and answer all questions. Slower than this rate means you may not be able to complete the test in the given time. If you are marking significant number of questions for review later, you need to target higher number per hour than this in the first 2-3 hours.

After test completion, review your answers. Look at the explanations for the ones you got wrong and also the ones you got right. To improve your understanding, you have to analyze each of your answers to see why the best choice is the best. Did you come up with the same reason to mark the correct choice or was it a fluke?

In terms of distribution and difficulty of questions, all the three tests are very similar to each other and the actual exam. So to see if you are making improvement, your score should get higher as you take the next mock tests.

Good luck!

2 - PMP MOCK TEST 1

200 Questions - Time Limit: 4 Hours

1. Which of the following is NOT an objective of the Control Risks process?
   A) Develop risk mitigation strategy
   B) Analyze contingency reserve
   C) Analyzing new risks
   D) Monitor risk triggers

2. A project manager wants to determine how his project is doing at the end of sixth month. The actual total expense of the project is $720,000. The planned budget for this length of time was $600,000. He finds that:
   A) The project is over-budget
   B) There is not enough information to determine how the project is doing
   C) The project is ahead of schedule
   D) The project is on track

3. Which of the following is an input to Manage Project Team?
   A) Work performance reports
   B) Work performance information
   C) Work performance data
   D) Work performance standards

4. An organization is highly reputed for deliverables quality. What would be an appropriate statement that BEST represents this situation?

A) The organization has a low cost of quality
B) Organization uses a standard quality management plan for all projects
C) Organization's project schedules are highly robust
D) The organization has a high cost of quality

5. All of the following are required to establish cost baseline EXCEPT:
   A) Plan Resources
   B) Control Costs
   C) Estimate Costs
   D) Determine Budget

6. Which one of the following is NOT an input to the Develop Project Charter process?
   A) Enterprise environmental factors
   B) Expert judgment
   C) Business case
   D) Statement of work

7. A project manager working on highway extension project finds out that noise barriers are required to be approved by the provincial highway authority before the work can proceed. The company does have a defined process and forms to go through the approval process. This defined process can be called as?
   A) Enterprise environmental factor
   B) A project
   C) Government requirement
   D) A program

8. What is a statement of work?
   A) A detailed description of deliverables to be produced by the project
   B) It is same as project scope
   C) The terms and conditions of the contract
   D) Work as defined in the project charter

9. If a project manager is working in a weak matrix organization, which of the following is INCORRECT?
   A) The project manager is not directly in charge of the project resources
   B) Only the project manager is responsible for the success or failure of the project
   C) The project team members report to functional managers

D) Functional managers make decisions that can affect the project

10. Which of the following is NOT an organizational process asset update during Close Project Or Phase process?
    A) Historical information
    B) Final deliverable
    C) Formal acceptance forms
    D) Project files

11. What is the Project Stakeholder Management controlling process called?
    A) Monitor and Control Stakeholders
    B) Control Stakeholder Performance
    C) Control Stakeholder Engagement
    D) Control Stakeholder Management

12. Which of the following is the BEST example of the use of coercive power by the project manager?
    A) Project manager asks a resource "Come on. You know you owe me. Get me the report tomorrow."
    B) Project manager talking to a resource "I want you to complete this report by end of tomorrow"
    C) Project manager says to a resource "If I do not get the document from you within two days, I will speak with your manager"
    D) Project manager asks a resource "Should I meet in person or just send her an email. Which is the right approach?"

13. Which of the following is not a type of risk attitude of organizations?
    A) Risk appetite
    B) Risk tolerance
    C) Risk response
    D) Risk threshold

14. You are the project manager for employee time management project. As part of the work, the project team is considering four different applications providing different functionality and reports. Which of the following will be your biggest concern?
    A) Schedule delay
    B) Scope creep
    C) Low quality
    D) Over budget

15. Right after you received final deliverable approval from the sponsor of

your project, you were assigned to a new project and asked to skip the closing processes for current project. For which kind of projects can you skip the closing processes?
   A) Large projects
   B) Administrative projects
   C) Closing processes should not be skipped for any kind of project
   D) Small projects

16. A project implemented several steps to improve customer satisfaction but the results from the next survey remained the same as before. How can the results be analyzed to find out why the steps did not make any improvement?
   A) Draw a control chart to see how many survey results are outside limits
   B) Using root cause analysis to find what is still causing customer dissatisfaction
   C) Create a Pareto Chart to see what is the biggest dissatisfaction customer is having
   D) Perform quality audit to verify quality measurements

17. You are mentoring a new project manager who recently started her career in project management. She wants to know which deliverable will provide her the criteria and guidelines to create and manage the project schedule. What will be your reply?
   A) Resource management plan
   B) Schedule baseline
   C) Schedule management plan
   D) Activity management plan

18. Results are recorded when a project goes through several iterations. Where should these results, when documented, benefit the project the MOST?
   A) Lessons Learned
   B) Issue log
   C) Project management plan
   D) Work performance data

19. A project manager uses all of the following management skills to coordinate towards accomplishing a goal EXCEPT:
   A) Public speaking
   B) Presentation
   C) Active listening
   D) Negotiating

20. You are the project manager of a network replacement project for a 40-floor office building. You plan to hire a contractor to pull the old cables out and then install the new cables. The work has to be done in such a way to have minimum to zero disruption to the tenant organizations during business hours, hence you need to hire a well experienced reputed firm. You contacted the procurement department to develop a list of firms that have the capability to do the work. What are you referring to?
    A) Develop evaluation criteria
    B) Negotiating a contract
    C) Solicitation package to be sent out to prospective sellers
    D) Qualified sellers list

21. In which process, for a medical research project running in two different regions, are the human resources engaged?
    A) Storming
    B) Acquire Project Team
    C) Develop Project Team
    D) Engage Resources

22. Disputes may arise between a buyer and a seller on a contract. There are several techniques that can be used to resolve such disputes. Which of the following is the sequence from most favorable to least favorable technique to be used?
    A) Litigation, Mediation, Arbitration, Confirmation
    B) Negotiation, Mediation, Arbitration, Litigation
    C) Negotiation, Escalation, Mediation, Arbitration
    D) Negotiation, Arbitration, Mediation, Litigation

23. One process in the Execution process group is where team member performance is tracked, appropriate feedback is provided and issues are resolved. This process is called _________.
    A) Manage Stakeholder Engagement
    B) Develop Project Team
    C) Monitoring and Controlling
    D) Manage Project Team

24. What happens in the Monitor and Control Project Work process?
    A) Planned work as per project management plan is completed
    B) Actual project performance is compared with the baselines
    C) Actual project performance is compared with cost performance baseline

D) Planned project performance is compared with the budget baseline

25. A project manager is managing three projects simultaneously. These three projects, A, B, and C are related to each other. Project A is to customize a software application X, project B is to deploy X to the whole organization and C is to train users according to their roles in X. How would you describe the situation?
   A) This is an operational work and should not be considered project
   B) He is managing one project which has three phases
   C) Project B should start after project A and Project C after Project B
   D) He is managing a program with three inter-related projects

26. A project's approved budget is $250,000 and planned budget to date is $150,000. What will be the Schedule Variance when Schedule Performance Index is 0.8?
   A) $50,000
   B) $30,000
   C) -$50,000
   D) -$30,000

27. You find it very valuable to attend the regular monthly project management training session. Most project managers at your office share your view and make effort to attend these sessions. It was mentioned in the last session that improvement in project management practice has been observed since the start of these training sessions a year ago. The PMO manager is quite pleased with these results because:
   A) Training, coaching and mentoring is one of the functions of PMO.
   B) Stage gate reviews can be scheduled to enable projects to proceed to next phases.
   C) Resources can be managed by project managers.
   D) More strategic projects can be initiated.

28. Which of the following is the project manager always responsible for?
   A) Meeting the project's profit margin
   B) Prioritizing projects based on business need
   C) Writing performance reports for project resources
   D) Selecting appropriate processes for the project

29. A project manager works with various stakeholders including negative

stakeholders mainly to overcome the resistance and gain the trust of those stakeholders. Which of the following skills did he use?

A) Management
B) Negotiating
C) Interpersonal
D) Writing

30. A project manager has been assigned to a project that is in trouble. He is going to focus his attention on:

A) Controlling procurements
B) Schedule because on-time delivery is most important
C) Communication because good communication ensures project success
D) Factors that have the biggest impact on meeting project objectives

31. For effective risk management, project risks __________.

A) Should be identified whether they are expected to have positive or negative outcome
B) Acceptance is the best strategy
C) Should be identified, analyzed and responded to
D) Should continue to be tracked even after it has occurred

32. Which of the following Project Communications Management knowledge area processes is part of the Monitoring and Controlling process group?

A) Plan Communications Management
B) Manage Communications
C) Control Communications
D) Managing Stakeholder Engagement

33. A project manager was asked by the project management office to make a presentation on project management to company employees in attendance. He made an incorrect statement about projects. Which one is it?

A) Current projects may have an impact on future projects in the same organization
B) Projects need to be elaborated as they progress
C) Completing projects on time and within budget always satisfies project stakeholders
D) Projects that do not get a project manager assigned formally may succeed

34. Which process identifies the ways to eliminate causes of unsatisfactory performance?
    A) Project Quality Management
    B) Control Quality
    C) Perform Quality Assurance
    D) Perform Quality Performance

35. You are the project manager of a building construction project. One of the routine meetings you have is a weekly meeting with project team where each team member provides you with how much work they have completed on assigned tasks and what are the measurements from quality tests. What are these examples of?
    A) Time and cost estimating
    B) Earned value analysis
    C) Perform quality audits
    D) Work performance data

36. In which process is the bidders' conference held?
    A) Control Procurements
    B) Plan Procurement Management
    C) Close Procurements
    D) Conduct Procurements

37. Acquiring, training, and managing team members that have been assigned to the project are part of which process?
    A) Direct and Manage Project Work
    B) Acquire Project Team
    C) Monitor and Control Project Work
    D) Manage Project Team

38. Organizational process assets that are updated during the Close Project or Phase process are:
    A) Project charter, business case
    B) Project management plan, expert judgment
    C) Project management plan, risk register
    D) Project charter, resource calendar

39. Your project has completed its 50% deliverables and is in the middle of execution. You created a stakeholder register during initiating process which was then used to create a stakeholder management strategy. You have been managing stakeholders according to this strategy. Now you have recently become aware of a highly influential stakeholder that has not been identified in the stakeholder register.

What is the BEST course of action?

A) Ask the project sponsor if this person be included in the stakeholder register
B) Send a request to senior management asking for direction
C) Update stakeholder register and stakeholder management strategy with the new information
D) Inform the stakeholder that it is too late for him to be involved in the project as the stakeholder register was completed during initiating process

40. You are the project manager for a system upgrade project. The practice at your company is to estimate project costs based on historical data and statistical analysis. This cost estimation technique is called:
    A) Analogous estimating
    B) Bottom-Up estimating
    C) Parametric estimating
    D) Risk based estimating

41. Which of the following is NOT a typical characteristic of a project management office (PMO)?
    A) Developing and managing project management methodology and standards
    B) Coaching and training project managers
    C) Managing project resources and assigning project tasks
    D) Defining and maintaining vendor engagement processes

42. The project schedule that you had submitted to the customer is not acceptable because the product delivery date is two months farther out than what the customer wants. Your company has a deep expertise in the subject area and several more resources are available that can be engaged by the project. What will you do?
    A) Crash the project schedule
    B) Fast track the project schedule
    C) Estimate activity resources
    D) Resource level

43. Which of the following processes best facilitates lessons learned document?
    A) Plan Communications Management
    B) Identify Stakeholders
    C) Perform Quality Assurance
    D) Plan Quality Management

44. An organization uses a desktop scheduling software for project scheduling. What would this software be considered as?
    A) Project management office
    B) Enterprise environmental factor
    C) Organizational process asset
    D) Integrated change control system

45. Which of the following is NOT a tool and technique for Control Schedule process?
    A) PERT analysis
    B) Resource Leveling
    C) Schedule compression
    D) What-If Scenario Analysis

46. What is the name of the technique that examines the problems experienced within the project, limitations faced, and the feeling of non-value-added work?
    A) Scatter diagram
    B) Quality audit
    C) Process analysis
    D) Quality assurance

47. The following are the goals of quality assurance EXCEPT:
    A) Confirm that project quality activities conform to quality policies and procedures
    B) Continuous quality improvement
    C) Verify project results comply with relevant quality standards
    D) Ensure appropriate quality standards have been setup for the project

48. As a project manager on a software development project for a customer, you have received an advice from customer that they want deliverable based invoices. This means you will have to track the costs by each piece of work done. The system within your organization is setup to capture costs by resources which means the total cost of the project at a certain instance is derived from cost booked against the project for the resources. What should you do?
    A) Only track costs as requested by customer
    B) Follow internal procedures and refuse customer
    C) Track costs both ways to fulfill internal and external requirements
    D) Evaluate to find out cost of complying with customer's demand

49. Which of the following normally provides the summary milestone schedule?
    A) Project requirements document
    B) Business case
    C) Project scope statement
    D) Project charter

50. A project schedule has activities and milestones. What do you know about milestones?
    A) Activities are summed up into milestones
    B) Milestones are required to create a valid schedule
    C) WBS work packages are also known as milestones
    D) Milestones can be a sponsor's requirement

51. Which of the following will have the BIGGEST impact in making project a success?
    A) Expert level technical knowledge
    B) Clear roles and responsibilities
    C) Co-located project team
    D) Highly experienced project manager

52. What is the output of a decision tree analysis?
    A) List of decisions that can be made
    B) Expected monetary value for each option
    C) Recommended corrective actions
    D) Cost of managing the risk that was analyzed

53. In order to calculate the estimate at completion (EAC), the following is typically needed:
    A) Cost performance index (CPI) and the actual cost (AC)
    B) Actual cost (AC) and the estimate to complete (ETC) the unfinished work
    C) Earned value (EV) and the actual cost (AC)
    D) Cost performance index (CPI), actual cost (AC), and the earned value (EV)

54. In a functional organization, what is the role of the project's sponsor during project execution processes?
    A) Managing integrated change control process
    B) Communicating with the project stakeholders
    C) Providing project status to management
    D) Helping the project manager resolve issues

55. Which of the following is the information about the group of stakeholders included in the project charter?
    A) Stakeholders who are very interested in the project
    B) Stakeholders who will be directly involved in the project work
    C) Stakeholders who are affected by the project
    D) Executive level stakeholders

56. Project stakeholders should be classified according to their interest, influence, and involvement in the project because:
    A) Such a classification makes it easier to assign responsibilities to stakeholders
    B) Project manager has limited time and it must be used efficiently
    C) Stakeholders need to know which group they belong to in terms of interest, influence, and involvement in the project
    D) Stakeholders usually have very little time to spend on the project

57. One of the following tasks is NOT part of the Control Procurements process. Which one is it?
    A) Review payment requests by the seller
    B) Answering questions of prospective sellers
    C) Resolve dispute occurring between buyer and seller
    D) Review performance of contract

58. You are managing a gas pipeline river crossing project. The project involves drilling piles in the river bed to build a bridge to cross the gas pipeline over the river. The biggest risk you have identified and planned a response for was the delay in shipping and import of steel piles from abroad. There were two shipments planned a few months apart. First shipment was received at the docks on time. Three large trailers took off from the docks to the site, carrying enough piles for three weeks of work. It will take them one week to reach the site from the docks. All the teams and installation equipment was ready on south bank of the river on the day the shipment was to arrive. The shipment reached the site on time but on the north side of the river. It would take a whole week to bring it to south side as the bridge which can accommodate the large trailers was very far from the site. No one in the project team had imagined this as a risk. What do you think will be the BEST way to handle this situation?
    A) Add this to risk register, analyze and develop risk response, then communicate to make sure no more trailers get sent to the north side
    B) This should be handled as an issue and not as a risk
    C) Evaluate impact of this issue on project performance baselines

D) Analyze this risk and use contingency reserve which is for unplanned risks

59. The project team has decided that a preventive action must be taken to solve an issue. What are they referring to?
    A) They are referring to an activity that can help eliminate performance of the desired state
    B) They are referring to an activity that can help lessen the chances of negative outcomes of actions
    C) They are referring to an activity that can help repair the chances of negative impacts
    D) They are referring to an activity that can help improve performance back to the desired state

60. What is the impact of noise on communication?
    A) Noise changes the message while being delivered
    B) Noise interferes with the understanding of the message by the receiver
    C) Noise impacts only if it is persistent
    D) Noise makes it hard to hear the communication since it is too loud

61. If you were to explain the difference between Control Quality and Perform Quality Assurance. Which of the following example explains it BEST?
    A) Control quality: measure the diameter of wheel to see if it is within limits. Perform quality assurance: Verify limits for wheel diameter are set correctly
    B) Control quality: Control the spelling errors in manuscript. Perform quality assurance: Assure that the spelling errors have been controlled
    C) Perform quality assurance: count number of books printed with reverse title. Control quality: count the number of titles reverse on the books
    D) Control quality: count nuts being produced. Perform quality assurance: count nuts being produced with defects

62. What do you call the aspects of the organization's environment that contribute to project risks?
    A) Events
    B) Conditions
    C) Impacts
    D) Historical records

63. As project manager, you can use a template to create ___________.
    A) Project Scope statement
    B) Risk management policy
    C) Requirements gathering
    D) Resource training procedure

64. You are working on creating the project charter for standard PC image development project. You have identified that the image must be ready for deployment by end of the year and the project must be executed with internal resources only. You will capture these conditions under:
    A) Constraints
    B) Assumptions
    C) Deliverables
    D) Scope of work

65. On a product development project, which is taking a totally new approach to product development unprecedented in the industry, what would be the BEST way to develop quality management plan?
    A) Use the quality management plan from last product development project that was completed successfully
    B) Take the old plan and add continuous improvement tool, stakeholder's required tests, and project team's preferred tests
    C) Create the plan from scratch in continuous consultation with stakeholders
    D) Delay the quality management plan until execution to ensure all requirements are fully defined

66. As the project manager you are going through the Conduct Procurements process of a project. The solicited prospective sellers' proposals have a significant price difference. What should you do?
    A) Verify if the statement of work and terms of the contract are clearly defined and unambiguous
    B) Award the contract to the best supplier
    C) Award the contract to the lowest bidder to get best value for the money
    D) Cancel the bid and re-advertise to solicit more bids

67. You are the project manager of a new human resources training system project. The project was late because of various reasons. Which of the following is a resource constraint on the project?
    A) A programmer was less experienced than expected
    B) A tester's per day cost was higher than expected

C) A developer was absent for 5 days due to sickness
D) Report specifications were not clear that resulted in rework

68. During a quality assurance audit, the audit team noticed that significant coding errors are occurring which are caught during testing phase. The defected code is returned for fix or rewrite, to the programmers. Three programmers have been replaced since the start of project for not being able to improve the code quality. On further drill down, the audit team found that most of the errors being reported are related to the nonconformance to company's coding standard. They also found that a training exists on company coding standards but the company policy says that training cannot be provided to temporary project resources and is only available to permanent employees of the company. What is the BEST thing to do?
A) Use internal trained programmers for this project
B) Prepare a quick presentation on company's coding standards based on the frequent errors observed and train the temporary project programmers
C) Recommend review of company's training policy
D) Ask that the training be waived for the programmers

69. A project manager for a global business expansion project lost a key resource on the project due to sudden illness. The resource is expected to recover in three weeks. Luckily the resource needs to start working on a deliverable exactly after three weeks. What is the BEST option for the project manager?
A) Add a three week contingency to the project schedule to cover up for absence
B) Immediately ask for a replacement resource
C) Take no action. Just keep in touch with the resource
D) Call the resource and let him know the importance of getting back on time

70. Which of the following organizational structure gives most authority to the project manager for a complex project involving multiple departments?
A) Balanced matrix organization
B) Functional organization
C) Strong matrix organization
D) Weak matrix organization

71. A project manager working for a government department is in the source selection process. He had advertised in the widely circulated

newspaper at a much higher cost than just inviting the six sellers of good reputation who have previously worked for his department. What can be the reason?

A) Get the best seller available in the market
B) Project manager is unaware of a cheaper solution of advertising through internet
C) Delay the process of awarding the contract to a seller
D) Government regulation requires public invitation to sellers for certain types of contracts

72. A project manager on a software development project used the quality management plan from his previous similar project which was very successful. What will be your advice to him?

A) It is customer's responsibility to provide the plan as they are the ones who know what quality is acceptable
B) Create a new plan for this project. Remember each project is unique.
C) Update the previous quality management plan keeping in view the uniqueness of this project, the customer's requirements and expectations
D) Reuse the plan as it has proved to be adequate for this type of project

73. Which of the following is an output from bid solicitation process in a project?

A) Award of contract to a seller
B) Prospective sellers' proposals
C) Create qualified seller list
D) Advertisement

74. All of the following are incorrect about the Validate Scope process EXCEPT:

A) It is concerned with acceptance of completed project deliverables
B) It ensures that project completes on time and within budget
C) It is concerned with meeting requirements to deliver business benefits
D) It is concerned with completion of change requests

75. You are managing a project that is near closing. The project team first went through the ________ stage and quickly moved into __________ stage, then passed through _________ stage to reach the __________ stage and stayed there. Now since the project is closing the team will go through _________ stage.

A) Forming, norming, storming, performing, adjourning
B) Forming, storming, norming, performing, adjourning
C) Forming, norming, storming, performing, adjusting
D) Forming, storming, norming, performing, adjusting

76. Project management plans are carried out when resources are coordinated. This is done in:
A) Resource leveling
B) Executing process group
C) Planning process group
D) Monitoring and Controlling process group

77. You were managing a project where a seller under a contract was executing some work. Due to performance issues, you decided to terminate the contract before completion. This triggers:
A) Closing Procurements process
B) Disputes
C) Controlling Procurements process
D) Negotiations

78. After performing risk analysis, you find that close to 50% of the risks are technology risks. What will you do next?
A) Develop a risk response strategy for all the risks that require a response according to plan
B) Develop a risk response strategy for all the technology risks that require a response according to plan
C) Acquire subject matter experts and highly qualified resources
D) Develop a risk response strategy for all the technology risks

79. Which of the following tool/technique includes Mind mapping and Affinity diagram?
A) Stakeholder analysis techniques
B) Group creativity techniques
C) Group decision making techniques
D) Observation techniques

80. What do you call the difficulties that can hinder the project team's ability to achieve project goals?
A) Assumptions
B) Risks
C) Constraints
D) Issues

81. Which of the following change management activities is NOT performed as part of the Perform Integrated Change Control process?
    A) Implementing the approved changes
    B) Identifying that a change has occurred
    C) Approving the requested changes
    D) Reviewing the requested changes

82. When customer is part of the team, which of the following tools and techniques is MOST valuable while performing probability and impact analysis?
    A) Detailed risk mitigation plans
    B) Risk register
    C) Customer's experience
    D) Expert judgment

83. Which process includes performing actions to execute the project management plan?
    A) Perform Integrated Change Control
    B) Direct and Manage Project Work
    C) Control Procurements
    D) Monitor and Control Project Work

84. In which of the following organizational structures, the project team members will be worried about their next engagement during the project close phase?
    A) Weak matrix
    B) Functional
    C) Projectized
    D) Strong matrix

85. Which two processes are parts of the Initiating process group?
    A) Develop Project Charter and Approve Project Charter
    B) Initiation and Develop Project Charter
    C) Develop Project Charter and Identify Stakeholders
    D) Develop Project Charter and Collect Requirements

86. _________ is any unique and verifiable product, result or capability.
    A) An objective
    B) A deliverable
    C) An action item
    D) An activity

87. There are several methods of forecasting project budget at completion.

Which of the following is NOT a forecasting method used on projects?
A) Time series
B) Program Evaluation and Review Technique
C) Judgmental
D) Econometric

88. All of the following are tools and techniques of Acquire Project Team process EXCEPT:
A) Negotiation
B) Acquisition
C) Networking
D) Multi Criteria Decision Analysis

89. Which document contains the information that describes how the formal verification and acceptance of the project deliverables will be obtained?
A) Scope management plan
B) Scope verification document
C) Communications management plan
D) Statement of work

90. You are in the Control Procurements process for your project. What is the Control Procurements process responsible for?
A) Define contract terms for optimum performance by the seller
B) Control the bidders' conference with appropriate controls
C) Manage the contractual relationship between buyer and seller
D) Creating and managing the statement of work

91. In which of the following stages of team development, the team members begin to work together and adjust their behaviors and work styles?
A) Performing
B) Storming
C) Adjusting
D) Norming

92. Thinking of communications planning for a global project with resources in different continents, which of the following is an example that BEST represents an assumption?
A) All resources are technically competent
B) Team members are acquired in various geographical locations
C) Costs in all countries is within budget

D) Entire team fluent in English language

93. You have been assigned to a project because the previous project manager left the company. You have found that the team morale is pretty low and team members seemed a bit reserved. Team is finding it difficult to complete deliverables. There were several other small issues too. What can you do to bring the team morale up and resolve other problems?
    A) Inform management that the previous project manager had failed to go through team development phases. Since you have to do it, extra time is needed
    B) Rebuild the team by redoing WBS and involving the team in re-planning of project. This will boost the morale of project team.
    C) Replace key team members and bring fresh enthusiastic resources
    D) Start afresh with building team, activating reward system, and clarifying roles & responsibilities

94. A project has 3 resources planned to work on the design for 6 hours/day each for twelve days. What will be the planned value of work on design at the end of eighth day?
    A) 48 hours
    B) 576 hours
    C) 144 hours
    D) 216 hours

95. When most of the team members of a project are working remotely, the benefits of co-location are lost. Which one of the following is the BEST way to manage such a team?
    A) Use instant messaging for real time discussions
    B) Bring all team members together for an offsite team building event
    C) Plan daily conference calls with the team
    D) Ask everyone to come in once a week to get some benefits of co-location

96. You are the project manager of a technology project and currently going through risk identification exercise. What does the Identify Risks process actually identify?
    A) It identifies what has happened in previous projects and still can happen
    B) It identifies what might happen on the project
    C) It identifies risks that are a risk to the project
    D) It identifies what will happen on the project

97. You are the project manager of a business process improvement project. The final deliverable was rejected by the customer. The team has identified a fix to the deliverable and is now working on it so that the deliverable can be resubmitted to the customer for acceptance. When the deliverable is accepted by the customer on resubmission, you will start which of the following process?
    A) Control Communications
    B) Validate scope
    C) Monitoring and controlling
    D) Closing

98. You were invited to a project management class at a community college as a project management practitioner. One student asked a question about budget spending and wants to know which process usually requires the biggest portion of budget. What was your reply?
    A) It depends on the type of project
    B) Executing process group usually spends the largest portion of the budget
    C) Monitoring and controlling group usually spends the largest portion of the budget
    D) Each process spends approximately same amount of budget

99. You are a project manager on a highway construction project. The project is on hold for last five days because of continuous rain and high winds but you are not worried at all about the project delay because you insured your project against delay due to inclement weather. How have you managed this risk?
    A) Mitigate
    B) Accept
    C) Avoid
    D) Transfer

100. For a technology project, in which process the project or a project phase is authorized to proceed?
    A) Initiating Process group
    B) Conduct Procurements
    C) Develop Project Charter
    D) Project Planning Process

101. You were managing a pharmaceutical project when suddenly the project sponsor, who was the head of laboratory, resigned from the company. The management immediately assigned his duties to another

person who became the new head of the laboratory and, by default, became the project sponsor. What is the MOST effective thing you can do?

A) Understand the communication needs of the new sponsor and update the communication management plan
B) Arrange a meeting and introduce yourself as well do a detailed review of the project
C) Provide him access to project repository and send him access information so that he may review the project records on his own schedule
D) Send him the project schedule, budget and scope details along with latest progress report

102. A project manager on a large scale laptop deployment project is doing reserve analysis. What is she comparing?

A) How much contingency reserve has been spent compared to how much management reserve has been spent
B) How much contingency reserve has been spent compared to how much is remaining
C) How much contingency reserve was spent on risks compared to how much was spent on other items
D) How much contingency reserve is still remaining compared to how much is the amount of remaining risk

103. As project manager you have to consider __________ which are factors that are believed to represent reality, considered to be certain and taken as truth.

A) Constraints
B) Assumptions
C) Risks
D) Deadlines

104. There is a document that is established through consultation and mutual agreement and that provides guidelines for common and repeated use. The objective of such a document is to make the repeated use more organized, reduce chances of error, and increase probability of success. It may also provide a minimum acceptable value of results. What is this document called?

A) Court order
B) Standard
C) Best practice
D) Regulation

105. You are the project manager for a technology implementation project. A change has been identified and needs to be presented to the Change Control Board (CCB). What do you know about the role and responsibilities of the change control board?
   A) Should have detailed contact information of all CAB members
   B) Should be clearly defined within the configuration control and change control procedures
   C) Should be clearly stated as part of project manager's role and responsibility
   D) Should be available on intranet site

106. A project manager suddenly resigned and left a project in the middle of execution. A new project manager assigned to the project found that the project was being managed without any control. No clear project organization existed and the deliverables were undefined. What will the new project manager do to organize the project?
   A) Perform lessons learned exercise and record all the learnings
   B) Create acceptance criteria for each of the deliverables
   C) Select a project life cycle and create roles and responsibilities chart
   D) Arrange re-kickoff project meeting to develop better coordination

107. What is the impact on project team development in a functional organization when the whole team reports to one functional manager?
   A) Team development is tedious and difficult to manage
   B) There is no need for team development in functional organization since everyone in the team already works in the same group
   C) Team development is much simpler ongoing process
   D) There is no impact on team development because team development is the same process no matter what the organizational structure is

108. A project manager is using risk management on her project. Why?
   A) To manage unknown risks
   B) To identify and analyze risks and then develop responses
   C) To manage uncertainty
   D) It is part of project management

109. Why is the change request an output of Validate Scope process?
   A) Change requests are the result of acceptance of deliverables by the customer in order to align scope with customer requirements

B) If a completed deliverable is rejected, a change request can be created to repair the defect
C) To ensure that all requested changes and recommended corrective actions are completed
D) Each change request has to be validated because it is considered complete

110. A procurement audit is a tool and technique that is used in ___________ process.
A) Control Procurements
B) Conduct Procurements
C) Close Project or Phase
D) Close Procurements

111. Where will you find the requirements for the Close Procurements process?
A) Statement of work
B) Terms of the contract
C) Procurement change control system
D) Enterprise environmental factors

112. The table below shows a schedule. Calculate the cost of crashing the schedule by seven days?

Activity	Duration	Predecessor	Cost of Activity	Cost of Crashing (per day)	Max Days it can be Crashed
A	7		2,000	200	0
B	9	A	3,000	200	2
C	8	B	2,000	300	2
D	9	C	4,000	300	3
E	5	C	3,000	500	3
F	4	D,E	1,000	100	0

A) $2,500
B) $9,000
C) $1,600
D) $1,900

113. You have realized that you have to crash few tasks in order to meet the external deadline. What is going to be your approach?
A) Crash tasks on critical path
B) Crash as many tasks as I can to reduce overall effort

C) Crash tasks that have the highest cost associated with them
D) Crash non-critical tasks to remove wasted time

114. The project quality management knowledge area explains quality that conforms to the concept given in all of the following EXCEPT:
A) Management by walking around
B) Failure mode and effect analysis
C) Plan-Do-check-Act
D) Six sigma

115. Which of the following is INCORRECT about the Control Scope process?
A) It clarifies scope to stop scope creep and disallow scope changes
B) It is the process of managing changes to the scope baseline
C) It evaluates the scope changes to understand the impact on the project scope
D) It is the process of ensuring all scope changes get processed through integrated change control process

116. Which of the following is an input to Identify Stakeholders process?
A) Plan Procurement Management
B) Plan Quality Management
C) Change log
D) Collect Requirements

117. You are working on a project and want to find out the list of projects that are closely related to your project and should actually be managed together with your project. You can find this information in:
A) Portfolio charter
B) Program charter
C) Strategic plan
D) Project charter

118. During the Define Activities process, constraints and assumptions are explicitly considered. What is considered implicitly?
A) Critical path
B) Defining activities
C) All information is considered explicitly
D) Deliverables

119. Which one, among the following, is the MOST useful place to see Estimate At Completion (EAC) and Estimate To Complete (ETC) information?

A) Cost performance data
B) Schedule performance data
C) Lessons learned
D) Forecast

120. Which one of the following is the main tool used in the Control Procurements process?
A) Contract change control system
B) Contract negotiation
C) Proposal evaluation criteria
D) Litigation

121. What type of time constraints impact schedule development and need to be considered in the Develop Schedule process?
A) Forced milestones and external deadlines
B) Scope and cost
C) Lead time and lag time
D) Explicit and implicit

122. A project manager has invited proposals from a list of qualified sellers to accomplish few deliverables of her project. She has created evaluation criteria in order to compare the proposals and select the best one. She is going through which of the following processes?
A) Conduct Procurements
B) Initiate Procurements
C) Control Procurements
D) Plan Procurement Management

123. Which of the following statements is INCORRECT about the level of authority of the project manager?
A) The project manager role is like a coordinator in weak matrix organization
B) In strong matrix organization, project manager's authority is that of a project expediter
C) A project manager has little or no authority in a functional organization
D) Project team members are under project manager in projectized organization hierarchy

124. A hospital wants to build a clinical information system (CIS) so a senior project manager was assigned to the three years long CIS project. It has several smaller projects starting and completing at different times. This is an example of:

A) A large project with multiple sub-projects
B) Phases of project life cycle
C) A large program with multiple projects
D) An Operational endeavor with multiple projects

125. You are a new project manager and have been assigned to estimate a project's costs. You go to a senior project manager who has been working in the company for 10 years and ask his advice. He asks you to increase your cost estimate by 25% since the management always cuts project budget by 25% before approving the project. What will you do?
A) Inflate each task's cost estimate by 25%
B) Present the actual cost estimate along with a brief explaining impact of a budget cut on the project
C) Add contingency reserve equal to 25% of the costs
D) Present the actual cost estimate along with a note that you will not manage the project if the budget is not approved as is

126. You are the project manager working on a project for an external customer. Which of the following will you NOT use to develop Project Charter?
A) Statement of Work
B) Signed Contract
C) Project performance baselines
D) Business Case

127. Which of the following is not a tool and technique of Manage Stakeholder Engagement?
A) Expert judgment
B) Communication methods
C) Interpersonal skills
D) Management skills

128. A project's current Schedule Performance Index (SPI) is 1.05. What is the project's schedule status?
A) Ahead of schedule
B) Behind schedule
C) Cannot be determined from SPI alone
D) On schedule

129. Which of the following is not an objective of Control Schedule process?
A) Analyzing activity durations to produce the project schedule

B) Influence factors that may have an impact on the project schedule
C) Manage changes to schedule baseline of the project
D) Find out if there is a change in project schedule

130. Which of the following is LEAST valuable as part of the contract?
A) List of deliverables
B) Terms and conditions
C) Roles and responsibilities
D) Work breakdown structure

131. You are managing an office space refurbish project. You are in the middle of negotiating the contract with a prospective seller. What is the primary objective of contract negotiation?
A) Push the seller to reduce the price
B) Pressurize the seller to do more work in the same price
C) Negotiate for better terms and conditions for the buyer
D) Develop a good working relationship and better understanding

132. A technology company is looking into four projects but can only execute one at this time. These are as follows: (1) An application enhancement project with an internal rate of return (IRR) of 10 percent (2) A system upgrade project with an internal rate of return (IRR) of 15 percent (3) A new market project with an IRR of 20 percent (4) A new product development project with an IRR of 25 percent. Which project should the company select?
A) New product development project
B) Application enhancement project
C) New market project
D) System upgrade project

133. During a regular project team meeting, one team member recommends a change to the product design that will though make it look cool but does not add to the functionality. The product is for internal use by the customer. The team agrees that if the customer is convinced of this change, it will not just enhance the product but also increases project scope, budget and time. Thus a secondary benefit is that the project organization will make more profit from this project and everyone on the project will be engaged for longer. One team member said "It is a win-win situation for all". Your company encourages upselling so this seems a good opportunity. What will be your response?
A) This is scope creep. You cannot allow this to happen to your

project.
B) Refuse to upsell something that does not add value in reality
C) Setup a meeting with customer to upsell the product
D) Evaluate budget and schedule impact before speaking with customer

134. Consider following characteristics: (1) Specific type of histogram (2) Ordered by frequency of occurrence (3) Shows defects by type. What is such a chart called?
A) Control chart
B) PERT chart
C) Pareto chart
D) Bar chart

135. Which of the following is a tool and technique for the Control Risks process?
A) Contingent response strategies
B) Meetings
C) Risk register updates
D) Corrective action

136. The table below contains work performance data from a project. Which activity has the best performance considering both schedule and budget?

Activity	Planned Value (PV)	Actual Cost (AC)	Earned Value (EV)
A	1,200	1,000	1,100
B	600	500	600
C	300	300	300
D	1,800	2,000	1,800

A) Activity B
B) Activity D
C) Activity A
D) Activity C

137. The contract was awarded to a seller who then started the work. The project manager assumed the role of contract administrator and started controlling the contract. Suddenly the management decided to cancel the project and thus terminate this contract. What is the FIRST thing the project manager will do?
A) Complete Control Procurements process
B) No action needs to be taken

C) Start Close Procurements process
D) Restart Conduct Procurements process

138. Your close friend, who is a project manager of a software development project that has the whole team co-located in one office, is having problems identifying a technique to use for team building. Which of the following will you recommend?
A) Send the technical team lead for training on 'working together in teams'
B) Install instant messaging application on each team member's computer
C) Arrange for all team members to participate in creating the WBS
D) Distribute contact information of project team members to the whole team

139. You are the project manager of a web development project. A seller was awarded a contract to build the dashboard to be integrated with the other web development work. Under the terms of the contract, the seller was required to produce a schedule of interviews with stakeholders for clarification of requirement. The schedule was to be approved by the buyer before the seller could proceed with the dashboard development. The seller instead had some informal discussions with few of the stakeholders that they have known really well from before. What should be your approach?
A) Issue the warning to the seller that if the schedule is not submitted immediately, the contract will be cancelled
B) Cancel the contract and award to the second best bidder
C) Ask the seller in writing to stop the work and submit the schedule for approval
D) Create a schedule and provide to the seller to move things along

140. An office renovation project is well underway. The sponsor being co-located makes frequent visits to work area. About 300 out of 400 desk areas have been renovated when he asks if another electric outlet could be placed on the right side of the desk in addition to the left side outlet. This is an example of _________.
A) Scope creep
B) Micro-management
C) Cost overrun
D) Schedule delay

141. A project manager wants to exceed expectations of his management. To achieve that, he has built aggressive schedules and tight budgets.

What is his risk approach?
  A) He is avoiding risks
  B) He is accepting risks
  C) He is transferring risks
  D) He is seeking risks

142. What is NOT an objective of controlling cost of project?
  A) Understand cost variances from baseline cost
  B) Establish cost baseline by including estimates
  C) Inform relevant stakeholders of all costs including change related cost
  D) Monitor completion of work and the money spent

143. Which process addresses actions and activities required to satisfy exit criteria for the project or phase? In other words, which process helps in confirming that the project has met all stakeholders' requirements?
  A) Stakeholder's define their needs and how these can be met
  B) Administrative closure procedure in the Close Project or Phase process
  C) Validate Scope
  D) Perform Quality Assurance

144. Which of the following factors in terms of use of the communication technology CANNOT generally affect the project?
  A) Urgency of the need for information
  B) Duration of the project
  C) Seller's proposals
  D) Project environment

145. A change request was approved by the change control board to fix project problem by bringing future performance of the project in line with the project management plan. Such a change request is called:
  A) Supportive action
  B) Corrective action
  C) Preventive action
  D) Submitted change request

146. Once the Perform Integrated Change Control process is completed, what is done next?
  A) Corrective actions are recommended
  B) Preventive actions are published
  C) Change request is closed
  D) Approved change is implemented

147. A large enterprise software development project requires that requirement documents be produced for each of the 18 departments. The project team created a checklist to control the quality of these documents. The checklist is filled out for each of the documents produced and is approved before sending it to the design team. The design team has identified issues with all 4 documents created till now. Which of the following is an appropriate action that should be taken?
   A) Inform the design team that it is too late for an objection since the documents have already been approved
   B) Review the quality plan, the completed checklist, and the issues identified by design team
   C) Reproduce the requirement documents so that the issues may not get repeated
   D) Share the completed checklists with design team to show that the quality standards set by the project were met

148. A project manager working on a project is identifying which project deliverables could be achieved from procurement through sellers. This project manager is in ___________ process.
   A) Control Procurements
   B) Plan Procurement Management
   C) Seller Procurements
   D) Conduct Procurements

149. A customer has asked you that he wants to review the completed deliverable before project moves to the next phase. Your response will be?
   A) Absolutely. Completed deliverables must be validated at end of each phase before project moves to next phase
   B) You cannot allow this until the project closing when customer has to validate completion of project work
   C) You can allow this only if the sponsor approves the customer's request
   D) The deliverables should have been reviewed by the customer as these were completed

150. Another project manager comes to you and asks for your opinion about a discipline problem he is having on his project. One of his team members is continuously being late to meetings and this is affecting project's progress. Your advice is to talk to the person in private and find out what is wrong. What type of power explains this scenario?
   A) Expert power

B) Formal power
C) Management power
D) Coercive power

151. What do you call the process that provides the seller with formal written notice of completion of a legal agreement?
A) Close Procurements
B) Close Project or Phase
C) Legal settlement
D) Control Procurements

152. What happens when a project manager involves project team members in project planning?
A) Project manager's time is saved because team members know what has to be done by the end of planning
B) It takes too long to plan the project
C) Clear scope definition results with an aggressive schedule to deliver
D) A more realistic achievable plan is developed

153. At the end of each phase of a business process streamlining project, a lessons learned review is held by the project team. The results of the lessons learned review are:
A) Published in the organization wide newsletter for the benefit of all employees
B) Distributed to each and every stakeholder for their information and feedback
C) Put into records of each team member to be used as part of their performance review
D) Kept confidential until the project is closed

154. A project manager had six team members during requirement gathering phase but the number increased to eleven in the design phase. How many additional channels of communication were added at design phase?
A) 40
B) 15
C) 25
D) 55

155. Project constraints can be all of the following EXCEPT:
A) Quality
B) Time

C) Template
D) Cost

156. You recently joined a company and were asked to take over a project in execution. First thing you did was to review all project documentation. You found that the project charter was approved by four sponsors. What will be your main concern?
   A) Managing project with multiple sponsors
   B) Identifying who will receive reports
   C) Identifying who will accept deliverables
   D) Communicating in a matrix environment

157. During an audit of a project in the middle of execution, the audit team found that some of the tasks were not done at the right time and in the proper sequence. What could be the reason for these anomalies?
   A) The Work Authorization System was either not established or is not working properly
   B) Communication plan does not exist
   C) Team coordination is poor
   D) Work breakdown structure does not exist

158. You work for a government department as project manager for technology projects. The change control board for your project meets regularly once a month and processes any submitted change requests. This month you had multiple change requests from various stakeholders that will impact time and cost. Luckily out of seven changes requested you have six that were approved. How will you proceed?
   A) Track approved changes against the cost and schedule baselines
   B) Update the business case and project charter
   C) Update cost and schedule baselines to reflect the changes
   D) Use work authorization system to make sure the change requests get processed

159. Project management processes differ from product oriented processes in that project management processes___________.
   A) are much more complex than product oriented processes
   B) ensure the project flows smoothly through to completion
   C) specify and create project's product
   D) have a definite start and end

160. Which of the following is the BEST action to increase acceptance of deliverables?

A) Offer discount on fees if deliverables are accepted quickly
B) Involve stakeholders during initiation
C) Send a written request to accept deliverables
D) Ask stakeholders to define deliverables

161. In a typical project, which of the following costs should be fully included in the budget?
A) All resources working on the project
B) All payments made to vendors
C) All project resources that are being charged to the project
D) All equipment used on the project

162. Which of the following processes include identifying new risks and monitoring residual risks?
A) Identify Risks
B) Plan Risk Management
C) Residual Risk Management
D) Control Risks

163. Which of the following skills is LEAST important for working as an effective project manager?
A) Body language
B) Active listening
C) Negotiating
D) Collaboration

164. Which of the following does these tools belong to? Filing systems, Electronic databases, Emails, and Web based project dashboard.
A) Information management system
B) Project deliverables
C) Project records
D) Project internal communication

165. All of the following are input to quality control process EXCEPT:
A) Deliverables
B) Project management plan
C) Pareto chart
D) Quality metrics

166. Can you calculate the cost variance (CV) of a project if, at a certain point in time, the actual cost (AC) is $19,500 and the earned value (EV) is $24,000? If yes, what is it?
A) yes. CV is -$4,500

B) yes. CV is 1.23
C) No. CV cannot be calculated from the information given
D) yes. CV is $4,500

167. You are the project manager for an application enhancement project. One of your designers is working very closely with the customer to ensure that the design meets all the customer requirements. During one session, the two of them changed the design of one deliverable that resulted in another deliverable being eliminated. This resulted in significant savings for the customer. You were not happy when you found out about this saving plan. Why?
   A) You were not included in the decision making
   B) Deliverables cannot be changed once baselined
   C) Scope control process was not followed
   D) The savings will result in reduced profit for your company

168. Which of the following is NOT a group decision making technique?
   A) Plurality
   B) Decision tree analysis
   C) Dictatorship
   D) Unanimity

169. A project deliverable has been formally accepted by the customer in the Validate Scope process. In which process this acceptance is documented?
   A) Validate Scope
   B) Close Project or Phase
   C) Control Procurements
   D) Perform Quality Assurance

170. When will the parametric estimating be considered most reliable?
   A) When considerable historical data is taken into account
   B) When expert judgment is used
   C) When estimating is done at activity level and then summed up for the project
   D) When estimating is done at higher level and distributed down to activities

171. You are the senior project manager on a new product development project. Your project management team includes a resource manager, a reporting manager, and a scheduler. You have advised the scheduler to build the schedule with the most common activity to activity relationship. Which relationship among the following are you referring

to?
A) Start-to-Start
B) Start-to-Finish
C) Finish-to-Start
D) Finish-to-Finish

172. You are the project manager for a manufacturing process improvement project for an automotive parts manufacturing plant. The hole size on one of the part was a big quality problem. The project identified the causes and fixes were put in place. Now you want to inspect the parts being produced to see if the fixes put in place have been successful and the parts being produced are within acceptable limits. Which of the following tools will you use?
A) Control chart
B) Fishbone diagram
C) Pareto chart
D) Scatter diagram

173. Influence/Impact grid is a tool and technique used in ___________.
A) Identify Stakeholders process
B) Plan Stakeholder Management
C) Manage Stakeholder Engagement
D) Control Stakeholder Engagement

174. In order to implement a quality assurance activity to supplement existing quality control activities, which of the following is the right tool for this purpose?
A) Benchmarking
B) Run chart
C) Expert judgment
D) Statistical sampling

175. Which of the following a project team should NOT do to manage stakeholders' expectations?
A) Determine the needs of stakeholders
B) Understand what are stakeholders' expectations from the project and the team
C) Deliver more than what stakeholders are expecting
D) Identify stakeholders throughout the project

176. A project management student, that you are mentoring, is confused about the benefits of work breakdown structure. You explained how the work breakdown structure is an input to many project

management processes. Then you mentioned all of the following processes as an example EXCEPT:

A) Sequence Activities
B) Define Activities
C) Estimate Costs
D) Plan Quality Management

177. You are managing a project as seller's project manager when you receive a request to add some work to the scope. Which type of communication is the optimum choice in this circumstance?
   A) Informal written communication
   B) Formal written communication
   C) Instant Messaging communication
   D) Formal verbal communication

178. Make or buy decision is an input to which process group?
   A) Planning
   B) Monitoring and Controlling
   C) Initiating
   D) Executing

179. Most of the project management skills are acquired as part of general management skills but there is one skill that is not generally a part of general management skills though it is required for managing projects for successful delivery. Which skill is that?
   A) Able to negotiate contracts with vendors
   B) A good listener that understands project related discussions
   C) Able to motivate and lead project team members
   D) Able to compromise and be flexible on any project related matter to achieve project goals

180. All the deliverables for your IT project have been accepted by the sponsor. These accepted deliverables are an input to the Close Project or Phase process. The deliverables were accepted through which process?
   A) Accept Scope
   B) Validate Scope
   C) Administrative closure
   D) Integrated change control

181. Solicitation of bids is part of the Conduct Procurement process. Who ends up putting the MOST effort in the preparation and advertising of bids?

A) Sponsor
B) Prospective sellers
C) Arbitrator
D) Project team

182. With ____________, potential problems are linked to various factors.
A) Cause and effect diagram
B) Quality assurance
C) Process analysis
D) Pareto chart

183. Which of the following is a best practice in the Plan Procurement Management process?
A) Procurement planning should start only after project management planning has been completed
B) Sellers who have failed to deliver in the past should be disqualified
C) Go through make-or-buy decision to analyze risks involved
D) Prefer fixed price contracts as these are less risky for the buyer

184. You are starting a new project as project manager. While talking to various resources you found out that one full time resource will be away on vacation for four weeks during project execution. What will you do?
A) Update Activity attributes of activities for which this person is a resource
B) Update the resource calendar with the information
C) Modify schedule baseline and critical path
D) Inform the resource that he cannot go away for four weeks in the middle of the project

185. You are the project manager of a clinical trial project. In project planning processes, what will you consider to understand how the costs will be managed?
A) Work performance data and project charter
B) Report format and level of detail
C) Business case and earned value measurements
D) Quality checklists and work performance data

186. A project manager who joined a new organization was asked to take over a project already in execution because the previous project manager suddenly resigned. She reviewed all the project documentation and uncovered several facts. The consolidated meeting

minutes revealed that very few meetings were held to update stakeholders on project progress. The issue log showed several open issues which had no status update. She could clearly see that the project significantly lacked proper communication. What can she do to make things right?

A) Create a communication plan that identifies what information is to be distributed and/or obtained and when this should happen. Then start implementing it.
B) Send an email to all stakeholders asking them to update the issue log as soon as possible
C) Perform a quality audit of the project to determine why such lack of information has happened on the project
D) Invite all stakeholders to a meeting and explain what has been missing

187. There are two recommended ways a schedule can be compressed. These are:
    A) Resource Leveling and Crashing
    B) Crashing and Schedule Networking
    C) Resource Leveling and Scheduling
    D) Crashing and Fast Tracking

188. Lack of complete information when moving from one phase of a project to another increases the risk of errors and rework. This may happen when phases are __________.
    A) Iterative
    B) Integrated
    C) Sequential
    D) Overlapped

189. As the project manager for a new project, you are in the middle of identifying stakeholders. Which process group are you in?
    A) Define scope process group
    B) Initiating process group
    C) Planning process group
    D) Create project charter process group

190. A project management office in a fast paced company is looking into establishing the practice of keeping historical records of past projects to help improve future project performance. The PMO can achieve this by mandating creation of:
    A) Lessons learned
    B) Project performance reports

C) Detailed project management plan
D) Detailed cost estimates

191. As project manager working for a seller of application development services, you had prepared a response to a bid invitation for executing a statement of work. The schedule and cost estimate was based on the premise that certain expert resources will be acquired and engaged for the project. After award of the contract, when you started to acquire the team, you ended up engaging resources with very little experience. The buyer had a serious objection to that. What should be the FIRST thing you should do?
    A) Submit a change request to update cost and schedule baselines to reflect reduced cost and delayed deliverables.
    B) Engage additional resources to cover up for low capability and to help the schedule stay on track
    C) Discuss with buyer what his concern is, and assure that the project will be completed within budget and on time
    D) Evaluate impact of resource capability on project cost and schedule

192. All of these are output of Direct and Manage Project Work process EXCEPT:
    A) Project charter
    B) Deliverables
    C) Change requests
    D) Work performance data

193. The products or services acquired through seller under a contract must meet the needs of the project and also must comply with business policies of the buyer. Who is responsible to ensure this compliance?
    A) Project manager
    B) The seller
    C) Project sponsor
    D) Legal counsel

194. Which of the following is CORRECT about the product scope?
    A) Product scope is the subset of project scope
    B) Product scope is a combination of product scopes of smaller components
    C) Product scope is the work needed to deliver the product on time, within budget and within scope
    D) Product scope and project scope are the same concepts. It is called project scope by the project team and product scope by

the customer.

195. Which of the following is LEAST challenging for virtual team members on a product design project?
    A) Reports
    B) Communication
    C) Team building
    D) Conflicts

196. Who cannot authorize a project?
    A) Sponsor
    B) Project manager
    C) Portfolio manager
    D) Project management office

197. __________ process uses earned value management to help understand performance variances in a project.
    A) Manage Communications
    B) Control Costs
    C) Direct and Manage Project Work
    D) Control Risks

198. The project manager just received a report that identifies two instances where the project plan is not following organization's standards. Which report is it?
    A) Project quality control report
    B) Project performance report
    C) Project quality assurance report
    D) Executive report

199. Which one of the following is NOT an objective of the Control Communications process?
    A) Create change requests
    B) Forecast the outcome of the project
    C) Develop cost performance baseline
    D) Analyze defects to recommend corrective action

200. The optimistic and pessimistic estimates for a major task are 24 and 12 days respectively. What is the standard deviation of this task?
    A) 1
    B) 2
    C) 12
    D) 4

3 - PMP MOCK TEST 2

200 Questions - Time Limit: 4 Hours

1. Which one of the following is an example of "halo effect"?
   A) Project manager received an award for project success though the whole team worked hard
   B) Project manager with strong technical knowledge was the reason for technical team's success
   C) Project manager creates such an environment that team members produce genuinely creative results
   D) A very successful programmer on projects was promoted as project manager

2. Mr. PM has been working on the enterprise learning management system project for 10 months with a fairly large team. Yesterday, the new system was made available to the whole organization with only one glitch viz. the mass email with incorrect login and password was sent out to all the employees. The project team worked on the issue diligently and within 4 hours sent out the correct email to everyone. Mr. PM met his manager on his way to the office this morning. The manager remarked "I am very disappointed". What could be the reason?
   A) Mr. PM did not go through Integrated Change Control Process to fix the issue
   B) Mr. PM did not mention his manager's name in the email sent out to the whole organization thanking the team for hard work
   C) The manager had received regular updates from Mr. PM on the preventive measures being taken to ensure email goes out

smoothly to the whole organization but still a supposedly prevented defect occurred
D) Mr. PM did not ask manager's permission if the problem should be fixed or not

3. What is Earned Value Management (EVM) commonly used for?
   A) Measuring project performance
   B) Analyzing the actual costs of the project incurred to date
   C) Measuring the expenses incurred by the project at a certain point in time
   D) Measuring the earned income by resources on the project to date

4. You are a project manager working on new product development project. You have a long-term contract with a reputed seller. Under the contract, the seller is charging you $50 per hour per resource engaged on your project and $200 per week as overhead charges. You have a ___________ contract with the seller.
   A) Cost reimbursable
   B) Fixed price
   C) Time and material
   D) Cost plus fixed fee

5. Coding software programs and testing of the code happens in which process group?
   A) Closing
   B) Monitoring and Controlling
   C) Executing
   D) Planning

6. You are working as a seller's project manager for a buyer on a cost reimbursable contract. The buyer wants to add scope to the current statement of work and also wants to change the contract to a fixed price one. You have all of the following options available EXCEPT:
   A) Since the buyer wants a fixed price contract, negotiate one that includes all the work that is still to be performed
   B) Negotiate a new fixed price contract for the additional scope but stay on cost reimbursable for the original statement of work
   C) Negotiate with buyer to restart the whole project with a fixed price contract so that a dispute can be avoided
   D) Refuse to do the additional work but complete the original work under the cost reimbursable contract

7. As project manager for a new product development project, you read a

report on hot consumer trends for the next decade. You realize that your product lacks some of those aspects. After review and discussion with the business and the marketing department, changes were approved to the product specifications. Why did this change occur?

A) Because an external factor has impacted your project
B) Because scope was not well defined
C) Because your project budget does not allow lavish spending
D) Because requirements were incorrect

8. You were invited to a meeting by a manager. When you entered the room you saw sitting there the key user working on your project. The manager tells you that she has discussed with the key user a change to the functionality being developed by your project: they both agree that it should be changed from manual entry to system generated entry. He then asks you to fill out the required form and get it signed. What is going on?

A) You are working as project expediter
B) The management is actively involved in the project
C) This is a good example of integrated change control
D) Manager is concerned with satisfying key stakeholders

9. When managing a medical research project, what should you focus on during the Executing processes?

A) Measuring progress
B) Performing the project work
C) Conflict resolution
D) Coordinating human and other resources

10. You are the project manager of a design build project that has an approved budget of $1,000,000. The project started eight months ago and has a total actual cost of $650,000 till now. The $650,000 is the:

A) Design cost
B) Earned value
C) Sunk cost
D) Cost variance

11. You have received a statement of work (SOW) from the customer. You will be using this SOW as an input when you are creating the project charter. Which of the following is NOT a reason why you received the SOW from the customer?

A) It was part of the proposal
B) You requested information from the customer
C) It was part of the contract

D) It was part of the scope statement

12. A project manager prepared the statement of work and developed the procurement management plan. He also has the bid package ready for distribution to the sellers. Which process does he go through next?
    A) Plan Procurement Management
    B) Control Procurements
    C) Conduct Procurements
    D) Procure Seller

13. You are a project manager working on a global project with project team members distributed in four continents. Which of the following can help you the MOST to be successful?
    A) Knowledge of local languages and customs
    B) Instant messaging & email
    C) Well developed virtual communication skills
    D) Responsibility Assignment Matrix

14. The difference between project lifecycle and product lifecycle is that:
    A) Project life cycle can span multiple product life cycles
    B) Project life cycle does not have a methodology while product life cycle follows a set pattern
    C) Project life cycle output is project while product life cycle output is product
    D) Project life cycle differs from industry to industry

15. A project was terminated in the middle of execution when half of the deliverables have already been completed. If you are the project manager of this project, what will you do?
    A) Discuss with the sponsor of what can be done to keep the project running
    B) Perform scope validation of the completed deliverables
    C) Stop the work immediately and release project resources
    D) Send a detailed project status report to the sponsor on how well the project was doing

16. If you have to choose one of the following as NOT being a project, which one will it be?
    A) Building a 10 ft. x 15 ft. shed in your backyard
    B) Creating a project management office in the IT department
    C) Increasing parking spaces from 300 to 400 in a parking lot
    D) Shipping 10 times larger than usual order received through internet

17. A project manager issued a purchase order to a seller to provide catering service during a major event. The event is three day meeting to be held for requirements gathering. The project manager is in which of the following processes?
    A) Plan procurement Management
    B) Close Procurements
    C) Conduct Procurements
    D) Control Procurements

18. If a project's actual total cost is $300,000 against a total budget of $400,000 and the project is 75% complete, then what is the earned value?
    A) Cannot be determined from the information given
    B) 0.75
    C) $300,000
    D) $100,000

19. Thinking about identification of stakeholders for a project, which of the following statements is incorrect?
    A) Project may get into trouble if negative stakeholders are ignored
    B) Stakeholders with a positive approach help project manager succeed
    C) Various stakeholders may have opposing views on a project
    D) Demands of positive stakeholders should have a higher priority than the negative stakeholders

20. Which of these is an input to the Control Quality process?
    A) Perform Quality Assurance
    B) Validated changes
    C) Deliverables
    D) Change requests

21. You being the seller's project manager are working on a project for a buyer. This was a small project with an unambiguous statement of work and well defined deliverables. You have completed all the deliverables as specified by the statement of work. Unfortunately the buyer does not like the deliverables and is quite unhappy. How should the contract be treated in such a case?
    A) Contract should be treated as complete
    B) Contract should be treated as cancelled
    C) Contract should be treated as if the work is still to be done
    D) Contract should be treated as pending

22. The Close Project or Phase process can be affected by various Organizational Process Assets. Which one of the following is NOT an Organizational Process Asset that can affect the Close Project or Phase process?
    A) Lesson learned knowledge base
    B) Project audits
    C) Marketplace conditions
    D) Transition criteria

23. Who is responsible for documenting project requirements and decisions about those requirements whether these are included in scope or not?
    A) Functional manager
    B) Project management team
    C) Customer
    D) Project sponsor

24. A project can have stakeholders from inside and outside of the executing organization. One of the following is not a stakeholder on a software development project. Which one is it?
    A) The workplace manager responsible for allotting office space to project team members
    B) The programmer writing code during the development phase
    C) The seller responsible for fixing broken chair and desk in the office
    D) The vendor performing third-party-testing of the code

25. Which technique will you use to engage a very hard to find expensive resource so that you can maximize the value?
    A) Leveling
    B) What-If scenario
    C) Fast tracking
    D) Pareto

26. You are managing an intranet development project for your company. During the design phase, one designer found a cool application that shows the stock value of the company in real time. As most of the employees own shares of the company, the team believed that this will be an extra value add to the scope of the project. What is going on?
    A) Delivery without proper testing
    B) Gold plating
    C) Nothing is going on

D) Exceeding expectations

27. Which of the following is true about constructive changes?
    A) Uniquely identified and documented through project formal communication
    B) Formal or informal change that can be implemented, without going through the integrated change control process, once the other party agrees
    C) Submitted by the seller to the buyer to improve the quality of bid
    D) Specific action oriented approved changes

28. You have just been hired by Company X as project manager for X31 project. You do not know the organization since you are new but you do need to start developing project charter immediately. What will be your initial focus while creating project charter?
    A) Business case
    B) Enterprise environmental factors
    C) Project team development
    D) Project management plan

29. A medical research project usually has a very fuzzy scope and a high degree of uncertainty. The BEST approach for such a project is:
    A) Iterative life cycle
    B) Intimated relationship
    C) Sequential relationship
    D) Predictive life cycle

30. One of your friends is starting his career as project manager and has been asked to manage a new project. He tells you that the organization has matrix structure and then asks you how the communication works in such environment. Your reply is that:
    A) Matrix structure means complex communication due to multiple channels of communication
    B) Matrix structure results in simple communication as project manager can communicate directly with most of the resources
    C) Matrix structure requires that communication with sponsor occurs on a regular basis
    D) All communication is efficient in a matrix organization

31. One of the resources on your project asks you that she has been assigned two tasks that have a 5 days lag between them and have a start-to-start relationship. What does that mean?
    A) Successor task will start 5 days after the predecessor task finishes

B) Successor task will start 5 days before the predecessor task starts
C) Successor task will start 5 days after the predecessor task starts
D) Successor task will start 5 days before the predecessor task finishes

32. How will you explain the concept of SWOT?
A) A devil's advocate in sheep's clothing
B) It is a special workers official team to handle complex issues
C) Expressed from 0 to 100 and converted to 0 to 1 for later calculations
D) An analysis of strengths, weaknesses, opportunities, and threats

33. Where will you determine project schedule constraints at a very high generalized level?
A) Scope Definition
B) Scheduling
C) Initiating
D) Planning

34. In a typical project, which of the following processes, from Project Time Management Knowledge Area, takes most of the effort?
A) Define Activities process
B) Control Schedule process
C) Develop Schedule process
D) Estimate Activity Resources process

35. All of the following are the tools used in the Control Quality process EXCEPT:
A) Control chart
B) Scatter diagram
C) Gantt chart
D) Pareto chart

36. A new project of computer deployment to the large global workforce in 90 countries received an approved budget in US dollars because the company's headquarters are in US. The cost of deployment in each country is different and has to be estimated independently. Which of the following challenges best represents this scenario?
A) Budget constraint
B) Scope creep
C) Cost estimation
D) Fast track schedule

37. A project manager is starting a new project. Which of the following he must do FIRST before proceeding with the project?
    A) Gather detailed requirements
    B) Create the Project Scope Statement
    C) Get the Project Charter approved
    D) Perform stakeholder analysis

38. Though all of the following techniques are used to solve problems in projects, which one do you consider to be the BEST?
    A) Rejecting
    B) Confronting
    C) Avoidance
    D) Compromising

39. What is the main objective of the Validate Scope process?
    A) Receive customer feedback
    B) Acceptance of work
    C) Start Project Close process
    D) Complete project on time and within budget

40. Which of the following is a tool and technique of Plan Scope Management process?
    A) Meetings
    B) Interviews
    C) Facilitated Workshops
    D) Decomposition

41. The sponsor is not happy with the project communication and has asked for a weekly progress update instead of the monthly one. Also he wants the update presented to him in a meeting rather than sent through the email. What should the project manager do?
    A) Inform sponsor that a weekly in person meeting is not possible since you also have to do the work
    B) Accept sponsor requirement and assign a project team member to present the progress report to sponsor in-person every week
    C) Invite a team meeting to discuss this new requirement from the sponsor
    D) Assess impact and if workable, update project communication plan by changing the monthly email to a weekly in person meeting

42. What would you call a measure that is implemented to bring future results in line with the project management plan?

A) A corrective action
B) A change request
C) A defect repair action
D) A preventive action

43. What is a work authorization system used for?
A) It is used to record activity attributes
B) It is used to manage project performance
C) It is used to manage resources working on the project
D) It is used to manage the time and in what sequence tasks are worked on

44. A project manager was managing the intercontinental high pressure gas pipeline construction project. The project was being executed using company's internal resources but needed to be fast tracked now. He looked at options and decided to quickly bring in a contractor to do the work. Since there is no time to issue a tender, he invited the contractor who had recently replaced plumbing in head office, and had done a really good job, to sign the contract. What did he miss?
A) Independent estimate
B) Request for proposal
C) Bidders' conference
D) Qualification of the seller

45. Which one of the following confirms that a communication has occurred?
A) The project manager has a consolidated minutes of meeting document
B) The project manager emailed the issue details to the sponsor
C) The project progress report was published in the company newsletter
D) The team member's performance improved after he came back from training

46. A project manager finds two of his team members in disagreement over the testing approach. The project manager met with the team members and ___________.
A) Asked them to write a change request so that formal decision can be made
B) Told them that arguing on petty matters can derail the project
C) Tried to understand what is causing the disagreement so that a solution can be suggested
D) Advised them to discuss in private as their disagreement is

damaging team spirit

47. You are the project manager of large construction project in a foreign country. The project employs over 300 unionized labors beside other resources and is expected to be complete in 8 years. The collective agreement is coming up for renewal later this year. You are preparing your project performance report and need to forecast project budget for the rest of the work to be completed. Which type of forecasting methods would be the BEST for this purpose?
    A) Judgmental methods
    B) Performance review methods
    C) Causal/econometric methods
    D) Time series methods

48. The quality audit team came back with their last month audit report. The report shows an increase in the number of non-conformances month over month. What steps can you take as project manager to find out the reason for this increase?
    A) Review the impact on the deliverable acceptance by the customer
    B) Use fishbone diagram to explore the root cause of the issue
    C) Recommend corrective action to improve the quality
    D) Send for training the project team member responsible for quality control measurements

49. A project manager is concerned about the performance of a team member. The team member has completed all of the assigned tasks later than the planned date and has not been able to provide a valid reason for that. The project manager sends him a notice of a meeting to discuss his performance in the presence of company's human resource representative. This is an example of what type of communication?
    A) Informal verbal
    B) Informal written
    C) Formal verbal
    D) Formal written

50. An output of Perform Quality Assurance is:
    A) Quality management plan
    B) Quality metrics
    C) Change request
    D) Quality control measurement

51. A phase end review identified that the deliverables completed as per

plan do not meet business need and are unacceptable by the customer. The next step can be:

A) Identify that change in business need is outside the control of the project and hence cannot be presented as an excuse to reject deliverables
B) Review if the project should be killed
C) Contact other stakeholders and ask for help
D) Inform customer that the deliverables are as per plan and must be accepted

52. What is the type of organization where an individual working as project coordinator does not have control over project resources? Instead those resources are managed by the functional manager.
    A) Functional
    B) Projectized
    C) Weak matrix
    D) Functional matrix

53. Control risks also includes updating the organizational process assets, __________________, for the benefit of future projects.
    A) Including fallback plan, alternative strategies and corrective actions
    B) Policies and procedures
    C) Including project lessons learned databases and risk management templates
    D) Quality improvement initiatives

54. Your colleague has been working as project manager on Human Resource Information System project. From the first month the project schedule started to slip and this has been the trend for last 6 months. Almost all deliverables have been late and the sponsor and end users are all disappointed. He told you, over a cup of coffee, that his reputation is on line and does not know what to do. You worked with him and used what-if scenario analysis to identify the factors that had impacted the schedule. After that you recommended him to:
    A) Add new activities into the schedule to cover for identified factors
    B) Redevelop project schedule with ample float to manage the identified factors
    C) Create change request to update the schedule baseline
    D) Send the list of factors to sponsor and end-user with an explanatory note

55. Which of the following is an attribute of project scope management?
    A) Project scope management is the same as project management as both deal with managing the project to success
    B) Project scope management defines the processes to enable the project to include all the work that is required (and only the work that is required) to achieve project's objectives
    C) Project scope management defines the scope, gathers the requirements and delivers the deliverables of the project
    D) Project scope management is the management of scope so that project can be completed on time, within budget and with high quality

56. What is the BEST statement to describe sensitivity analysis?
    A) Estimates how risk tolerant the stakeholders are for the project
    B) Estimates the impact on one variable by changing all other variables
    C) Estimates how risk tolerant the project team is compared to the rest of the stakeholders
    D) Estimates the impact of changing one variable when all other variables are kept constant

57. You are managing your first project at a company. This is a system upgrade project that happens every 2-3 years for last 10 years. In order to estimate costs you are consulting the cost performance baselines and lessons learned from those projects. Which technique are you using?
    A) Ball Park estimating
    B) Parametric estimating
    C) Analogous estimating
    D) Bottom-Up estimating

58. A system of awarding team members for exceptional performance is an excellent motivator. If the criterion to win the reward is too hard to achieve, it has a reverse effect. The team motivation can actually go down. Which motivational theory presents this idea?
    A) McGregor's Theory of X
    B) McGregor's Theory of Y
    C) Expectancy Theory
    D) Maslow's Hierarchy of Needs

59. In which type of organization the following resource problem can occur? A project manager is unable to get his resource request accepted by the infrastructure manager because all resources are

engaged in other projects. The only way he can get resources is to escalate the issue one level up to the director.
   A) Strong matrix
   B) Functional
   C) Projectized
   D) Weak matrix

60. You are the project manager on an RFID research project. The project is in planning process and you are estimating the project costs. The team has come up with an estimate of $750,000 using parametric estimating technique. A senior project manager in the company gives his opinion that the project should not cost more than $500,000. Which estimate will you use?
   A) $750,000
   B) $500,000
   C) $625,000
   D) 1,250,000

61. Due to resource shortage in the market and within the organization, a project manager has fewer resources available than what he requested for his project. Which technique will he be using if he adds buffers to the project so that the project completes on the planned date?
   A) Critical chain method
   B) Resource allocation
   C) Resource leveling
   D) Resource breakdown structure

62. A project manager who is working on a retail banking project for a large financial institution has developed a project management plan. He believes it is a realistic plan and thus should be formally approved. Which of the following organizational assets will not have impacted the development of the plan?
   A) Organization's change management policies
   B) Project management plan templates
   C) Business case for the project
   D) Lessons learned of a previous project

63. Where can the following be found?
  1) Project life cycle selection
  2) The processes to be applied to each phase, and
  3) The results of project management processes tailoring
   A) Project schedule
   B) Risk management plan

C) Project charter
D) Project management plan

64. What is the concept of watch list in risk management context?
    A) List of identified risks that have risk response planned and watched to see if it actually occurs
    B) List of resources whose performance is being watched for corrective action
    C) List of scope items from the project scope that are risky
    D) List of identified risks that are watched to see if their probability or impact changes to warrant a response

65. If a scatter diagram shows majority of points around the diagonal line on the chart, what does this tell you?
    A) Variables are closely related to each other
    B) Variable trend is increasing as the time progresses
    C) Variables are independent of each other
    D) Factors affecting the chart are resulting in a straight line relationship which is an indication of nonconformance

66. An internal application deployment project is running into trouble. Too many errors have been reported by the users. Which of the following tools should the project manager use to see the frequency and types of issues being reported?
    A) Pareto diagram
    B) Control chart
    C) Scatter diagram
    D) Run chart

67. Which of the following is not a work performance data?
    A) Costs incurred
    B) Deliverable status
    C) Stakeholders list
    D) Schedule progress

68. Analytical techniques is a tool & technique of which of the following processes?
    A) Sequence Activities
    B) Estimate Activity Durations
    C) Define Activities
    D) Plan Schedule Management

69. The project cost baseline should include all of the following EXCEPT:

A) Material costs
B) Management costs
C) Equipment costs
D) Labor costs

70. A project manager, who is working on a custom house project, has been asked by the customer to make a change to the dining room size. What is the BEST way of communicating with the customer on this issue?
A) Formal written
B) Informal written
C) First Informal written then formal verbal
D) Formal verbal

71. All of the following statements are correct about portfolio management EXCEPT:
A) A portfolio serves strategic goals of an organization or department
B) Success of portfolio cannot be determined from success or failure of just one of many projects and programs within it
C) A portfolio has a start and end date just like project and program
D) A portfolio can have projects and programs

72. You are the project manager of an enterprise application time tracking project. Your project requires several changes to meet customer needs, stay on schedule and within budget. You have a system to manage and control these project changes. Each of the proposed change goes through an analysis of the impact of that change on the project scope, deliverables, cost and schedule. A change is either approved or rejected. Stakeholders may be notified, if needed. What helps you achieve all that?
A) Configuration chart and Cost control
B) Control chart
C) Change control and Control board
D) Configuration control and Change control

73. You are managing a corporate training system project. You have to present on a monthly basis project performance review to the senior management stakeholders including the project sponsor. Which of the following will NOT be part of the information presented?
A) Issues that need management attention
B) Forecast of when project will be completed
C) A team member's performance issues

D) Superior performance by project team and the results

74. In which process group will you create a list of all of the people who will be directly affected by the project?
    A) Executing
    B) Initiating
    C) Identify Stakeholders
    D) Planning

75. The project you have been managing has run into problems lately. During code testing, several issues have been identified that require significant amount of work to fix. You need additional resources to stay on track and complete the project on time. Your formal request to add more resources has been approved by the sponsor. What will be your next step?
    A) Review project scope to identify changes
    B) Modify the schedule baseline
    C) Request funds from management reserves to pay for the additional resources
    D) Close the identified risk

76. A structured review of the procurement process is performed by reviewing procurement from the Plan Procurement Management through the Control Procurements to identify what went well and what did not. What do you call such a review?
    A) Negotiated settlement
    B) Procurement audit
    C) Procurement review
    D) Performance review

77. A customer rejected a deliverable, which was submitted by the project team for acceptance, with the objection that it does not meet requirements. The team believes that the deliverable fully meets the requirements. What is the FIRST thing the project manager should do?
    A) The issue requires a confronting approach followed by a forcing technique to resolve the problem
    B) Review the acceptance criteria and the deliverable then consider arguments presented by both customer and project team
    C) Submit a change request to resolve the discrepancy
    D) Customer is always right. Ask the team to make the change

78. Which of the following information you will not see when you are

looking at a composite resource calendar?

A) Hourly rate
B) Non-availability
C) Competence level
D) Experience level

79. If scope is being added to a project that is already executing, additional risks must be identified. Correct this statement.
    A) If scope is being added to a project that is already monitoring and controlling, additional risks must be identified
    B) If scope is being withdrawn from a project that is already executing, additional risks must be identified
    C) If scope is being added to a project that is already executing, new risks will occur
    D) If scope is being added to a project that is already executing, risk identification should be performed

80. Total Quality Management can be explained as:
    A) The planning that results in reducing the defects to one part per million or less
    B) A business philosophy to find methods that will continuously improve products, services, and business practices
    C) The process to ensure Plan-Do-Check-Act process is carried out
    D) Quality management planning that results in end to end quality product from project results

81. A project manager on a large project submitted the project charter to the sponsor for approval and stated that the project will be divided into three phases. Each phase will start with initiating process. The project manager plans to use those subsequent initiating phases to:
    A) Ensure all approved changes get implemented
    B) Fulfill the requirement to go through all the project process groups on the project
    C) Help keep the project aligned to meet the business needs
    D) Close the previous phase and start the next phase

82. While managing a project with resources working in two countries, a project manager receives two resumes for an open position in the other country. One candidate is the team leader's son who barely meets the requirement and another person who is well experienced. The preferred practice in the country is to hire immediate family members before hiring from outside. What should the project manager do?

A) Replace the team leader before hiring the experienced resource
B) Hire the team leader's son if every other criterion is met
C) Leave the decision to team leader because he is ultimately responsible for getting the work done
D) Hire the experienced resource to get maximum productivity out of this role

83. Which of the following is NOT considered a characteristic of team building?
A) Team building activities can be done remotely
B) Team building activities can be done formally and informally
C) Team building activities should continue throughout the project
D) Team building activities should be work related

84. If a project manager finds himself in a position where an external team is about to start the quality audit of the project but the internal team is against such an audit in the middle of the project, what should be his approach?
A) Inform the team that quality audit will help identify inefficient and ineffective policies and procedures
B) Request the audit team to delay the audit until end of the project so that the project team can focus on completing work on time
C) Inform the team that quality audit will verify the time sheets submitted by the team members to ensure compliance with company policies
D) Inform sponsor about team's concern and ask for direction

85. A project manager is having problems with attendance in the team meeting. One member is too busy with the project work and another dislikes meetings. Both of them never bother to show up. A highly experienced senior project manager is asked to help the project manager identify a solution. The senior project manager recommends that a meeting notification be sent out in advance identifying that attendance is mandatory and leave of absence must be taken in advance from the project manager. Which power is the senior project manager referring to?
A) Expert
B) Referent
C) Formal
D) Coercive

86. ___________ is a structured, independent review to determine whether project activities comply with organizational and project

policies, processes, and procedures.

A) Customer audit
B) An organizational audit
C) A quality audit
D) Senior management review

87. You are managing a tunnel boring project in a remote area. You have a choice to either buy or rent a mole (boring machine). If you buy it, you will pay $150,000 lump sum price but also incur $5,000 per month for its maintenance. If you rent it, you will pay $10,000 per month and an additional one-time administration fee of $5,000. How many minimum months you have to use it to justify buying it rather than renting it?

A) 15 months
B) 30 months
C) 29 months
D) 16 months

88. A project manager created a simple status report for his project. The report was in a dashboard format showing performance information including percent complete, above, at or below planned. What is this information for?

A) It shows how much work each project resource has completed and how is his/her performance against the expected performance
B) It shows schedule, budget, and scope. Their % complete and status of where actual stands vs. planned
C) It shows % completed work by the seller and actual rating against the expected rating
D) It shows project manager's performance vs. other team members' performance

89. The project manager received a letter from the vendor's representative. Who is the decoder?

A) No one
B) Project manager
C) Letter
D) Vendor's representative

90. You are managing a building construction project. The project is at a stage where you are spending most of the budget and managing maximum number of resources. The level of influence stakeholders can exert in this phase compared to earlier phases has:

A) Stayed the same

B) Reduced
C) Reduced for project sponsor and increased for rest of the stakeholders
D) Increased

91. ___________ can be obtained through one-on-one meetings, interviews, survey, and/or focus group.
A) Quality assurance results
B) Project progress report
C) Expert judgment
D) Stakeholder list

92. Disputes occurring in a project that is being executed under a contract are common. These disputes can be related to scope, price, schedule, quality, resources, etc. Which of the following is the preferred method of resolving these disputes?
A) Mediation
B) Arbitration
C) Negotiation
D) Small claims court

93. Which of the following rules for effective meetings helps the MOST in order to stop everyone talking at the same time, being non-participative, and discussing random points?
A) Advise all in attendance to discuss one topic at a time
B) Reduce the number of people in the meeting. Invite only those that are participating
C) Publish an agenda before the meeting and set ground rules for the meeting
D) Make participation mandatory when inviting for the meeting

94. ______________is the cost management process that aggregates the estimated costs of individual work packages.
A) Control Costs process
B) Determine Budget process
C) Estimate Costs process
D) Plan Cost Management process

95. Which of the following four best describes the type of process quality assurance is?
A) Measurement
B) Management
C) Inspection

D) Controlling

96. You are about to complete a project with resources in a matrix environment. One of the activities you will be doing is to release the project resources. Which of the following is NOT an example of releasing the resources?
    A) Engaging resources on another project
    B) Return of the rental equipment
    C) Writing performance report of individual resources
    D) Transfer of individuals to various departments

97. A software development project has teams defined by project phases. There is a requirement team, design team, development team, and testing and deployment team. Each of these is responsible for work in a separate phase. What will identify transition from one phase to another within the project's life cycle?
    A) Milestones
    B) Handoff
    C) Project reports
    D) Deliverables

98. All of the following can be used as historical information for cost estimating EXCEPT:
    A) Commercial cost estimating databases
    B) Project files
    C) Knowledge of individual project team members
    D) Already approved project budget

99. What is still left to be done when final product has been accepted by the customer?
    A) Procurement closure
    B) Scope validation
    C) Lessons learned
    D) Earned value

100. Which of the following is an input to the Define Scope process?
    A) Project scope statement
    B) Requirements documentation
    C) Product analysis
    D) Requirements traceability matrix

101. Which of the following is NOT part of the project scope statement?
    A) Project objectives explained in detail

B) List of activities that must be completed to achieve project's objectives
C) List of deliverables that must be produced by the project
D) Project requirements that must be met by the project deliverables

102. ____________ is responsible for the quality of the project deliverables for a building construction project.
A) Seller
B) Sponsor
C) Quality assurance team
D) Project team

103. Which of the following is an INCORRECT statement about project and/or product life cycle?
A) Customer views project life cycle as product life cycle
B) Conception, business case, product, operations, and end of life define product life cycle
C) Several project life cycles may fall under one product life cycle
D) A product life cycle may end at the same time as project life cycle

104. Which of the following is a characteristic of a project team in a projectized organization?
A) Team members report to functional managers
B) Each team member has multiple reporting relationships
C) Team members report directly to the project manager
D) Team members are never co-located

105. You are a project manager of an airport construction project. You have analyzed risks and found that a risk has changed. Which process group are you performing?
A) Perform quantitative risk analysis
B) Identify risks
C) Control risks
D) Perform qualitative risk analysis

106. A supplier, under a contract, is working on part of your project. For your project, the contractual provisions of that contract can be considered as:
A) Risks
B) Constraints
C) Provisions
D) Changes

107. Your project is in the middle of executing phase. You were in a meeting with the sponsor when he mentions a concern. This is a risk that has not been identified before and recorded on the risk register. What are you going to do?
   A) Inform the project team what this risk is about
   B) Explore this risk further with the sponsor and alleviate his concerns
   C) Identify on the risk register and analyze that risk
   D) The risk identification process was already over so this concern can be ignored

108. The PMO manager advised a new project manager that risk identification is one part of a continuous process. Risk identification continues throughout the project followed by risk analysis of new and existing risks. These risks are then tracked. The PMO manager is talking about ____________ process.
   A) Identify risks
   B) Direct and Manage Project Work
   C) Plan Risk Management
   D) Monitor and Control Project Work

109. Validate Scope process is an essential scope management process. When is it performed?
   A) At each phase end
   B) At project end
   C) At Monitoring and Controlling process group end
   D) At project start

110. All of the following are attributes of the control charts EXCEPT:
   A) Shows relationship between two factors or objectives
   B) Stability of a process can be observed
   C) Shows measurements plotted against time
   D) Results of a process can be monitored

111. You, as the project manager, are discussing with management that a project management methodology should be used since it helps the project succeed. As a first step you told them that you will create a project charter because you believe it will help you:
   A) Get more authority as project manager
   B) Create a strong business case
   C) Get the project charter approved
   D) Identify all stakeholders

112. What is the main objective of schedule control process?
    A) Measure schedule variances from baseline schedule
    B) Apply approved changes to the baseline schedule
    C) Minimize changes to the project schedule
    D) Control changes to the project schedule

113. There are four kinds of dependencies when sequencing activities. These are mandatory, discretionary, internal, and external. Which type of dependencies are fully documented since they can create arbitrary float values and can later limit scheduling options?
    A) Floating
    B) Preferential
    C) Environmental
    D) Fixed

114. A project has Cost Performance Index of 0.6. All activities were completed on time except one work package. This work package was for design work and could not be done because the expert resource was unavailable till now. Now the project manager has to calculate the estimate to complete for the remaining project work. Which approach will he take?
    A) Use original planned rate of progress
    B) Use current rate of progress
    C) Use current rate of progress for design work package and planned rate of progress for rest of the work
    D) Create a totally new estimate

115. What is the difference between quality and grade?
    A) Quality is how many features are in the product while grade is how much the features of the product perform to the specification
    B) Quality and grade are the same thing
    C) Quality is what is measured in Quality Control process and grade is what is measured in Quality Assurance process
    D) Grade is how many features are in the product while quality is how much the features of the product perform to the specification

116. The figure shows a network diagram with values given as per the legend in the diagram. What is the Late Finish (LF) date of activity D?

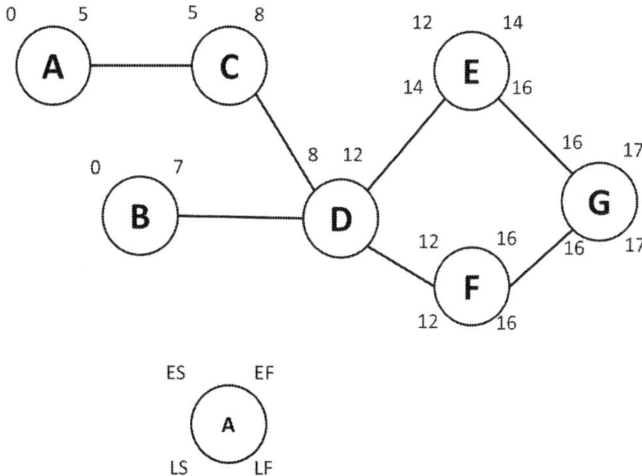

A) 16
B) 12
C) 8
D) 14

117. Resource Calendars are an output of Acquire Project Team process. Which of the following information is NOT provided by a resource calendar?
   A) Location and contact information of resource
   B) Vacation time of resource
   C) Resource schedule conflicts
   D) Engagement period of resource

118. Which one of the following is an output of Direct and Manage Project Work process?
   A) Project deliverables
   B) Project management plan
   C) Project forecasts
   D) Project charter

119. Which of the following CANNOT be derived from the work breakdown structure?
   A) Project's cost estimate
   B) Project objectives
   C) Project's resource need
   D) Work packages

120. What is the relevance of project performance appraisals for project team members?
    A) Team that performs well is praised well
    B) Review of an individual team member's performance on the project
    C) Project performance as appraised by a third party impacts how project team members are valued outside the project
    D) Review of overall project's performance is considered an individual's performance

121. A project manager could not decide how to plan a project which has various stakeholders with different objectives and needs. What can he do to bring all stakeholders to a common understanding and combined objectives?
    A) Remove from the project all the stakeholders that have a negative approach to the project
    B) Use focus groups/brainstorming sessions/objective discussion among project stakeholders to reach a common ground
    C) Ask the sponsor to identify which stakeholders should be satisfied
    D) Document each stakeholder requirement and rank from most favorable to least favorable for the project

122. Which of the following is NOT an advice you will give to your project team members in regards to managing project stakeholders?
    A) Understand stakeholders' needs and expectations
    B) Focus on project work and let the project manager worry about continuous stakeholder identification
    C) Understand the influence stakeholders can put on the project, identify how project impacts them
    D) Whenever a stakeholder is identified, it should be recorded on the stakeholder register

123. How does quality relate to the project scope?
    A) Quality, whether stated or implied, is to meet the needs by completing the scope
    B) Quality meets the scope by completing the needs whether stated or implied
    C) Quality is the measuring of scope of a project
    D) Quality exists to satisfy project scope

124. You joined a new company where projects are assigned to each project

manager at the start of fiscal year. The project manager is responsible for completing all projects by the end of the year. It is his/her responsibility to prioritize the project execution. You were assigned four projects, A, B, C, and D project. You started working on project A and while it was in executing process, you initiated project B. Both projects were running concurrently. Project A was a small system upgrade project but scope of project B has been expanding since initiation. You find it difficult to manage project B. While going through project repositories you found a similar project executed two years ago. What will be your line of action?

A) Complete project A as soon as possible and do not get engaged in project C or D until project B is done
B) Put project B on hold until project A is completed
C) It is important to define the requirements completely. There is no need to feel overwhelmed.
D) Review project documents of the previous project and discuss challenges with its project manager

125. Only one of the following statements is CORRECT about the work breakdown structure (WBS). Which one is it?

A) WBS is a method to distribute work to various resources so that project can be completed successfully
B) WBS is a hierarchical decomposition of the work to be executed by the project team
C) WBS is the list of project deliverables that must be agreed in writing by the sponsor to move project forward
D) WBS is a hierarchical list of project activities shown under each department

126. Which of the following tools and techniques will you use to determine which change requests should be approved among several requests that are recommending preventive and corrective actions?

A) Monte Carlo simulation
B) PERT analysis
C) Earned value technique
D) Expert judgment

127. If one has to estimate intended cost of the project for the purpose of comparing with cost estimates so that significant anomalies can be identified, which tool would be the BEST?

A) Independent estimates
B) Bottom-Up estimating
C) Procurement audit

D) Bidders' conference

128. Your management has asked you to review a troubled project and suggest the best course of action. The project is expected to be completed one week later than the baseline completion date. Though the project has a low risk, the Internal Rate of Return is expected to be 15% which is very promising. A closer review of the schedule reveals that most dependencies built are discretionary. You asked management about resource availability to find out if more resources can be engaged to speed up the work but was told that no resources are available. What do you suggest?
    A) Change discretionary dependencies to lags
    B) Move resources from non-important activities to major activities
    C) Remove few non-critical activities to reduce the schedule
    D) Fast track schedule

129. The project team is working on estimating activity durations for the Next Generation Tablet Development project. The team has mix of resources with no experience to expert level experience. The estimates provided for tablet assembly range from 4 hours to 12 hours. There seems to be a consensus that most likely it will take 10 hours to assemble the tablet. In this situation, you have no choice but to use Program Evaluation and Review Technique (PERT) to determine how long it will take to assemble the tablet. You found out that it will take ______ hours.
    A) 8
    B) 9
    C) 12
    D) 26

130. Which one of the following is the BEST choice to explain how much of the project management processes should be applied in a project?
    A) All processes must be rigorously applied to ensure project success
    B) At minimum the core processes must be applied. Rest depends on the rigor required by the project sponsor or PMO
    C) Appropriate processes and the level of implementation should be selected to meet project objectives
    D) Project manager, as the subject matter expert in project management, should make the decision to how many processes should be applied

131. An environmental cleanup project has been completed. There are

strict requirements imposed by the government as environmental issues are very sensitive. To make sure all of the requirements are met and an audit is cleared without a hitch, you want to engage environmental experts that are luckily available within your company. You are considering __________ for closing the project.

A) Organizational process assets
B) Enterprise environmental factors
C) Scope Validation
D) Expert judgment

132. Which of the following is not an input to determine the project budget?

A) Activity cost estimates
B) Project schedule
C) Agreements
D) Reserve analysis

133. You are a project manager working in a functional organization. One of your project team members is upset because he is overloaded with work request by others. He should be assigned work only by the __________.

A) Sponsor
B) Project manager
C) Project team members
D) Functional manager

134. Which of the following is NOT a type of cost-reimbursable contract?

A) Cost plus award fee
B) Cost plus fixed fee
C) Cost plus material fee
D) Cost plus incentive fee

135. Which one of the following is NOT a function that is typically performed by the project sponsor?

A) Lead project status review meeting
B) Clarify scope
C) Communicate with executives
D) Influence project decisions

136. A project had a list of identified risks. This list was in the risk register. Where can one find the high-level risks?

A) Project charter
B) Risk management plan

C) Risk register
D) Project management plan

137. What will happen if too many changes occur throughout the project life cycle?
    A) Project will not meet the targets
    B) Team morale will be lower
    C) Stakeholders dissatisfaction will be the result
    D) Frequent project re-planning happens

138. You are working on an HR process streamline project. The subject matter expert (SME) that was supposed to work on your project was reassigned to a high visibility project which has CIO as the sponsor. What action will you take?
    A) Demand that the resource be allocated back to your project since the resource was assigned first to your project
    B) Determine the impact this decision will have on your project
    C) Compress schedule so that you can manage the project without this resource
    D) Put in a request to hire a consultant to fill the SME role

139. As project manager of an application development project, you were in a meeting with the customer where your developer was displaying the newly developed report. The report showed the names of the employees who have not completed their mandatory training. You also saw the date of start of employment displayed against the name of the employee, which you knew was not part of the requirements. The customer was happy with this new information and believed this will help with the purpose of the report. What happened here?
    A) Benefit realization
    B) Scope creep
    C) Project success
    D) Exceeding expectation

140. How much role nonverbal communication, such as facial expressions and hand gestures, play in sending a message and how it is received?
    A) More than 50 percent of the message is nonverbal
    B) 25 to 50 percent of the message is nonverbal
    C) 5 to 10 percent of the message is nonverbal
    D) 10 to 25 percent of the message is nonverbal

141. Advertising as a tool is generally used in which of the following process?

A) Control Procurements
B) Conduct Procurements
C) Close Procurements
D) Plan Procurement Management

142. Is Work Performance Information an input, output or tool and technique of the Control Communications process?
A) Input
B) Output
C) Tool and Technique
D) None of these

143. Which of the following can be a reason to update project performance baselines of a tunnel boring project?
A) Some rework was done which cost the supplier additional $40,000
B) A change request to increase the overall cost of the project by $50,000, due to change in the price of drill bits, has been approved
C) Electrical contractors just bought a new machine for $500,000 to use on the project
D) Supplier is adding more resources to the project on a fixed price contract

144. A project manager was struggling with managing team meetings. Some issues he noticed were: late to meeting, leaving the meeting room without any indication, missing a meeting without notice, taking mobile phone calls during meeting, and occasional texting. What can the project manager do to improve the situation?
A) Set new ground rules that address the attendance, behavior and distractions issues
B) Request sponsor to join a meeting and motivate the team
C) Get the team out on a team building exercise to develop the team spirit
D) Advise members of serious consequences if they do not behave

145. There are two ways a contract can be closed. One way is by completion of the contract. What is the other way?
A) Sublimation of the contract
B) Incompletion of the contract
C) Closure of the contract
D) Termination of the contract

146. You have been assigned as project manager for a human resources process improvement project. While performing stakeholder analysis, you identified one stakeholder who is an expert in domain knowledge which has been marked risky for the project. This stakeholder has high interest in the project but very low influence due to his position in the organization. Which would be the best approach?
   A) Keep him informed and solicit his feedback on risks and issues
   B) Manage this stakeholder closely
   C) Monitor him so that he could be managed closely if he becomes influential
   D) Keep him satisfied by sending him regular project performance reports

147. What is configuration management system?
   A) A system that configures the project for better management and provides management reports for such configuration
   B) A System that describes the process of controlling the project management processes and methods to actually control these processes
   C) An encompassing system that includes integrated change control and project management information systems
   D) A System that describes items requiring formal change control and provides the process for controlling changes to these items

148. How will you differentiate between Direct and Manage Project Work process and Monitor and Control Project Work process?
   A) Monitor and Control Project Work process is part of the Direct and Manage Project Work process
   B) Both processes are the same
   C) Direct and Manage Project Work process reviews the project performance while the Monitor and Control Project Work process is concerned with performance of work
   D) Direct and Manage Project Work process is concerned with performance of work while the Monitor and Control Project Work process reviews the project performance

149. You have been assigned to a project that is expected to have a large number of stakeholders but you do not know who they are. What would be the BEST way to identify all those stakeholders?
   A) First identify all stakeholders then record them on the stakeholder register
   B) Use stakeholder analysis matrix to pinpoint all stakeholders
   C) Use Salience Model to identify all stakeholders

D) First identify main stakeholders and then expand the list with their input

150. In which process is the resource histogram created?
    A) Develop Project Team
    B) Plan Human Resource Management
    C) Manage Project Team
    D) Acquire Project Team

151. A project manager finds that the reason for a sponsor's worried communications about the project work is because there are several issues recorded in the issue log have not been updated since last month. No one seems to be working on those as there is no update shown. What should the project manager do FIRST?
    A) Increase the frequency of communication to stakeholders especially sponsor
    B) Review open issues, update issue log and take steps to get those resolved
    C) Perform a performance review of the team member responsible for the delay
    D) Send an apology note to the sponsor and assure that issue log will be regularly updated from now on

152. After performing Quantitative Risk Analysis process, what happens to the risk register?
    A) Risk register gets updated with risk response plans
    B) Risks on the risk register gets prioritized
    C) It is continuously updated to reflect the changes
    D) Risk register is archived as historical record

153. A buyer has rejected a deliverable that was submitted for acceptance by the seller. The buyer has cited the specific term of the contract under which the deliverable has been rejected. On a closer review, the seller's project manager agrees with the buyer. Among the following, what is the BEST option for sellers' project manager?
    A) Review the requirements and option to fix the deliverable or recreate the deliverable
    B) Put in a request to change the referred term of the contract
    C) Review the referred term of the contract with the legal counsel
    D) Identify team member responsible for the error and take disciplinary action

154. Which of the following types of risks can generally have both positive

and negative outcomes?

A) Injury
B) Business risks
C) Life risks
D) Fire and theft

155. What type of contract is most commonly used when the product specifications are very detailed, precise and well-defined?

A) Cost-reimbursable
B) Time and material
C) Time lapsed
D) Fixed-price or lump-sum

156. Why is the contingency reserve not included in the cost estimate?

A) Because it will overstate the cost estimate, if included
B) Because it can deplete the management reserve
C) Because it will maintain the management reserve
D) Because it will understate the cost estimate, if included

157. Which of the following is an input to the Manage Stakeholder Engagement process?

A) Project Management Plan
B) Change requests
C) Change log
D) Work performance data

158. Which of the following is NOT an objective of the Close Procurements Process?

A) Validate procurement deliverables
B) Update and archive procurement records
C) Handover the final product of the project to the customer
D) Create or update lessons learned document

159. You have just come out of a project meeting where all the team members discussed what went well and what didn't with the project. All the points were written down in a document. This project is in which process?

A) Executing
B) Monitoring and controlling
C) Closing
D) Planning

160. Which of the following is NOT a characteristic of the cost

performance baseline?
   A) It shows cumulative approved budget against time
   B) It is used to monitor and control cost performance of project
   C) It is typically displayed in the form of an S-curve
   D) It is derived from schedule performance baseline

161. Which of the following is the MOST important point to understand an argument between two individuals?
   A) Facts and fiction in the arguments
   B) What time of the day, early morning, close to end of the day
   C) Pitch and tone of the voices and body language
   D) Expertise level of the individuals on the subject matter of argument

162. During the Conduct Procurements phase, who generally takes the lead role negotiating contracts for project work?
   A) Project manager
   B) Procurement specialist
   C) Project sponsor
   D) Functional manager

163. Which of the following options is NOT an objective of the kick-off meeting?
   A) Roles & responsibilities clarification
   B) Gathering requirements
   C) Project team introduction
   D) Stakeholder involvement

164. If a project is late and there is a need to compress the schedule to complete the project on time without reducing the scope, which technique can be used?
   A) Forecasting the schedule
   B) Crashing the schedule
   C) Fast Tracking the schedule
   D) Analyzing the schedule

165. Which of the following is an input to Perform Qualitative Risk Analysis process?
   A) Quality Management Plan
   B) Activity Duration Estimates
   C) Work Breakdown Structure
   D) Cost Management Plan

166. A project team was trying its best but was unable to meet the specification of the product. Project manager decided to analyze the variance and decide proper course of action. Which process will that be in?
    A) Executing
    B) Initiating
    C) Integrating change control
    D) Monitoring and controlling

167. What is the advantage the Precedence Diagramming Method has over other network techniques?
    A) It provides a graphical view of dependencies among activities
    B) It is the most commonly used technique
    C) It shows the project start and finish dates
    D) It shows project progress at any point in time

168. Which of the following is an input to Managing Stakeholder Engagement process?
    A) RACI chart
    B) Work breakdown structure
    C) Change log
    D) Management skills

169. Which of the following tools and techniques can be used to close a project or a phase really well?
    A) Expert judgment
    B) Project management information system
    C) Administrative procedures
    D) Procurement audits

170. You being the project manager of Fertilizer Plant Extension project are reviewing the schedule developed for your project. You goal is to determine the project end date based on schedule analysis of least flexible activities. Which tool are you using to perform this analysis?
    A) Ishikawa diagram
    B) Precedence Diagramming Method (PDM)
    C) Critical Path Method
    D) PERT analysis

171. As project manager you have gone through risk identification exercise with the project team and other stakeholders. The result was a comprehensive list of identified risks recorded on the risk register. Next, you created an online survey with the identified risks as

questions, requiring answers in the form of probability and impact. You ask all stakeholders to go online and fill the survey. The responses are confidential so no one knows who else filled the survey and no one can see others response. Which of the following techniques you have used?
   A) Risk analysis
   B) Risk identification
   C) Delphi Technique
   D) Risk response planning

172. Direct and Manage Project Work process has various inputs, outputs, and tools and techniques. Which of the following is none of those?
   A) Approved change requests, project charter, and project management information system
   B) Project management information system, work performance data, project management plan updates
   C) Approved corrective actions, approved preventive actions, and expert judgment
   D) Deliverables, hiring and firing guidelines, change requests

173. You are the project manager of a large construction project where over 200 resources are working. The project accountant is unsure about the cost center of one particular resource. Which of the following is the BEST tool that can help in this situation?
   A) Bottom-Up estimating
   B) Resource leveling
   C) Scope Validation
   D) Work Breakdown Structure Dictionary

174. Why a risk has a very low score when its probability of occurrence is very high?
   A) Impact has high value
   B) A calculation error
   C) Impact has not been assigned yet
   D) Impact has low value

175. Risk register can be BEST described as _______________.
   A) A register that is used to check-in and check-out risks for response planning
   B) A document that contains all of the outcomes of risk management processes
   C) A document that identifies risks so that responses can be planned
   D) A document that contains list of identified risks

176. One of the stakeholders on your project has been identified as having high power, low urgency, and appropriate legitimacy (involvement in the project). Which classification method did you use?
    A) Influence/Impact grid
    B) Power/Interest grid
    C) Salience model
    D) Power/Influence grid

177. The Close Project process will be started by all of the following EXCEPT:
    A) Project has been cancelled
    B) Project plan was rejected
    C) Project sponsor has stopped supporting the project
    D) Project is significantly late

178. Stakeholder register is an output of Identify Stakeholders process and an input to:
    A) Develop Project Charter
    B) Plan Procurement Management
    C) Organizational process assets
    D) Plan Quality Management

179. If you were to find out the longest time between planned start and finish dates of a project, which tool will you use?
    A) Business case
    B) Work Breakdown Structure
    C) Project charter
    D) Network diagram

180. If there is an approved change to a project that affects the project budget, what will you update to reflect the change?
    A) Integrated change control system
    B) Project charter
    C) Project's Earned value
    D) Project's cost performance baseline

181. What does corrective action mean in regards to risk response?
    A) These are two different things. Corrective action is related to change while risk response is to risk
    B) It means putting the planned risk response into action
    C) It means correcting the risk response on a continuous basis
    D) It means creating risk response that suggests corrective action

182. A project manager has used Affinity diagram method to review and group large number of errors being reported on the project. He is planning to further analyze and identify the root cause of errors. What is he doing?
    A) Perform integrated change control
    B) Brainstorming
    C) Perform quality assurance
    D) Decision making

183. Which of the following is NOT a tool used in the Control Communications process?
    A) Expert judgment
    B) Information management system
    C) Forecasting methods
    D) Meetings

184. One of the following is neither an input to nor an output of the Develop Project Charter process. Which one is it?
    A) A business need
    B) A project charter
    C) A project statement of work
    D) Project management plan

185. Which of the following is an input to the Closing Process Group?
    A) Quality control measurements
    B) Change request
    C) Work Performance reports
    D) Accepted deliverables

186. Which of the following is an Alternative Dispute Resolution (ADR) technique?
    A) Lithigation
    B) Mediation
    C) Collaboration
    D) Escalation

187. What is the difference between Close Procurements and Close Project or Phase?
    A) Close Procurements requires the return of all property back to the buyer
    B) Close Procurements must happen before Close Project
    C) Close Procurements can be repeated for each phase of the

project within the same contract
D) Close Project or Phase involves customer but Close Procurements does not

188. A project manager is in the process of gathering seller's responses, selecting a seller and then awarding the contract. This process is called conduct procurement and is part of _______ process group.
A) Planning
B) Monitoring and Controlling
C) Executing
D) Control Procurements

189. Kaizen method is the same as:
A) ISO9000 method
B) Just In Time
C) Continuous improvement
D) Marginal analysis

190. Your latest report says that by the end of last week your project had Earned Value (EV) of $127,200 and Planned Value (PV) of $143,000. You are going to present that report later today. How will you explain in simple terms how is your project doing?
A) Cannot be determined from the information given
B) Ahead of Schedule
C) Behind Schedule
D) Exactly On schedule

191. All of the following are examples of cost of quality EXCEPT:
A) Performing additional tests before deployment
B) Review and acceptance of requirement document by the key users
C) Responding to a user request for defect repair
D) Hiring a truck to move material closer to the site

192. Several change requests, for your mall development project, analyzed by the project team for impact on the project and then submitted to change control board, have been approved. What will you do next?
A) Inform project team that the changes have been approved
B) Implement the change requests
C) Revise project plans and baselines with the changes
D) Inform stakeholders that the change requests have been approved

193. You are the project manager of documentation project which is part of an enterprise program. Currently, you are developing the criteria of source selection for your contract. Source selection happens in which process?
   A) Request Seller Responses
   B) Plan Procurement Management
   C) Conduct Procurements
   D) Develop Project Management Plan

194. A work breakdown structure was created for the auto parts plant manufacturing project. The team reached a point where they were able to identify 75 work packages. The work package information was sent to various departments for review. All departments were content with the level of detail for their work package but the store department objected that the work packages are too high level and should be sub-divided into smaller manageable packages so that accurate estimate can be prepared and detailed schedule can be developed. The team identified a technique that will be used to fulfill this request. Which technique is it?
   A) Work packaging by type of resources instead by department
   B) Rolling wave planning
   C) Discretionary planning
   D) Analogous estimating followed by Parametric estimating

195. When is the BEST time to do a lessons-learned identification exercise?
   A) Throughout project life cycle
   B) At the end of the project
   C) As soon as a lesson is learned
   D) At the end of each issue or failure

196. During negotiation, with the customer about the work to be performed and effort involved, the customer objects to the effort being proposed on quality control and quality assurance processes. As the project manager, which one of the following concepts you will explain to the customer to remove the objection?
   A) Cost of conformance vs. cost of nonconformance
   B) CMMI audit requirements
   C) Quality assurance and quality control
   D) Continuous improvement focus

197. How will you differentiate between the project plan and the project baseline?
   A) Project plan changes as project progresses while project baseline

is frozen once created

B) Project plan can be changed at regular intervals while project baseline can be changed anytime

C) Project plan is used for executing the project while project baseline is used for measuring performance

D) Project plan and project baseline are the same. There is no difference

198. Which one of the following is NOT a forecasting method to predict future project performance?
    A) Earned value
    B) Linear prediction
    C) Control chart method
    D) Regression analysis

199. Which of the following would be the LEAST preferable way to classify stakeholders?
    A) High influence, Medium influence, Low influence
    B) Internal, External
    C) Executives, Managers, Staff
    D) Supporter, Neutral, Resistor

200. You are the project manager of a straight forward technology deployment project. The project is expected to be completed in one year by deploying the technology on all the computers in the company. How often are you going to perform risk identification?
    A) At a regular frequency throughout the project
    B) At the start of project only since it is a simple project
    C) At start of the project and just before deployment as that is the most critical time when whole company becomes stakeholders
    D) At the start, middle and end of the project as it is a simple project but a bit long

4 - PMP MOCK TEST 3

200 Questions - Time Limit: 4 Hours

1. All of the following are correct statements about the contract change control system EXCEPT:
   A) Buyer and seller both can submit a change request to the contract change control system
   B) Contract change control system is mainly used during the Control Procurements process
   C) Contract change control system should be defined separately from the terms of the contract
   D) Contract change control system is a part of the project's integrated change control system

2. All of the following can be the responsibilities of a project management office (PMO) EXCEPT:
   A) Developing and maintaining centralized projects repository
   B) Training, coaching, mentoring, and evaluating project managers
   C) Developing and managing project management standards
   D) Gathering detailed requirements, creating project charter and developing project management plan

3. The Control Schedule process in Time Management knowledge area uses all of the following tools and techniques EXCEPT:
   A) Resource optimization techniques
   B) Modeling techniques
   C) Leads and lags
   D) Expert judgment

4. What is the purpose of reviewing a defect repair? Which of the following BEST describes defect repair review?
   A) To ensure the defect was repaired properly and as required
   B) To ensure stakeholders are satisfied with the repair
   C) To create a Pareto chart to see the major reason for defect
   D) To verify the extent of the repair as per scope defined in the project charter

5. Which of the following BEST describes the difference between project management process groups and project life cycle phases?
   A) Project phases are repeated in project management process groups but may also continue from one project management process group to another
   B) Project management process groups are used in waterfall while project phases are used in iterative
   C) Project management process groups are repeated in project phases
   D) Project management process groups and project phases are the same thing

6. On a Power/Interest grid, the project sponsor should typically fall in which group?
   A) Monitor
   B) Keep satisfied
   C) Manage closely
   D) Keep informed

7. You are managing a project that is in the middle of developing a project charter. You will use one of the following as an input for developing project charter. Which one?
   A) Project performance baseline
   B) Work performance information
   C) Project scope statement
   D) Organizational process assets

8. What is effective communication in a project context?
   A) A message is decoded by receiver, then received by the sender who encodes the message in the presence of some noise
   B) A message is sent by encoder, received by decoder, then sent back by encoder, and received by decoder
   C) A message is encoded by coder, then sent to the decoder who decodes a noise

D) A message is encoded by sender, then sent to the receiver who decodes the message in the presence of some noise

9. You are working in a Projectized organization. Which of the following title you will have when you are in a project manager role?
   A) Project facilitator
   B) Project manager
   C) Project expediter
   D) Project coordinator

10. If you are looking at the work performance data to determine the project's performance, what should you do NEXT?
    A) Update the lessons learned document
    B) Identify areas of improvement and create corrective actions
    C) Send the information to project sponsor
    D) Compare the information with baselines and identify variances

11. You have a seller working on a Time and Material contract. As per contract, two resources will work for 12 months on the project for a total cost of $180,000. However, the project took longer than expected and by the time it was completed, the two resources have been on the project for 18 months with a total cost of $250,000. What went wrong?
    A) Just like an incentive for finishing earlier, a penalty should have been proposed for delay
    B) A maximum amount and time limit should have been established under the contract
    C) Fixed price contract which is good for these kind of situations, should have been used
    D) Nothing went wrong since this was Time and Material contract under which resources charged for the time they worked on the project

12. If the project is behind schedule, the earned value is:
    A) Less than the Planned Value (PV)
    B) More than the Actual Cost (AC)
    C) Less than the Actual Cost (AC)
    D) More than the Planned Value (PV)

13. A project manager is working on office space refresh project. While using earned value technique, he determines that the project will run over budget by $2,000 if current performance trend continues. The project manager has used ____________ characteristics to identify the

issue.
   A) Interpersonal
   B) Knowledge
   C) Problem solving
   D) Earned value

14. Which project management process will you use if you find out that the tasks needed to accomplish a work package are not valid?
   A) Integrated change control
   B) Corrective action
   C) Preventive action
   D) Monitoring and controlling

15. Which of the following is NOT an input to the Plan Procurement Management process?
   A) Work performance data
   B) Project scope statement
   C) Work breakdown structure
   D) Stakeholder register

16. An electronic mail is what type of communication?
   A) Formal electronic
   B) Formal written
   C) Informal nonverbal
   D) Informal written

17. Success of which of the following is measured in terms of benefits realization?
   A) Operations
   B) Portfolios
   C) Programs
   D) Projects

18. You are managing a construction project. Your team took a sample of wet concrete and sent it to the laboratory for testing the quality. Which project management process is your team performing?
   A) Perform Quality Inspection
   B) Perform Quality Sampling
   C) Perform Quality Assurance
   D) Control Quality

19. What is an output of the Close Procurements process that the buyer provides to the seller?

A) A copy of the lessons learned document
B) Written notice of acceptance of all deliverables and completion of contract
C) Project management plan updates
D) Letter of appreciation to the seller

20. As project manager of a system upgrade project, you have engaged your project team members, and are going through activities to improve team interaction. Which process group are you in?
A) Monitoring and controlling
B) Initiating
C) Executing
D) Planning

21. Which of the following is INCORRECT about conflicts?
A) Conflicts should be resolved publicly to avoid any misunderstanding
B) Conflicts happen all the time
C) Most conflicts can be resolved using a collaborative approach
D) Conflicts should be attended to earlier than later

22. What does consultants and professional and technical associations provide during project execution?
A) Deliverable status
B) Work performance data
C) Expert judgment
D) Issue management procedures

23. A project manager has just started a new project and going through initial meetings with sponsor and other key stakeholders. One Vice President (VP) who is a key stakeholder wants to know how much the project will cost and how long it will take. The project manager has just initiated the project and does not have details but still provides an estimate to the VP. Which technique did he use?
A) Parametric estimate
B) Analogous estimate
C) Bottom-Up estimate
D) Ball Park estimate

24. Which of the following is an input to Control Stakeholder Engagement process?
A) Work performance report
B) Work performance information

C) Work performance data
D) Work performance analysis

25. A common way of representing the stakeholder management strategy is a ________________.
    A) Communication strategy
    B) Stakeholder register
    C) Stakeholder analysis matrix
    D) Power/Interest grid

26. Which information flows from Direct and Manage Project Work process to Develop Project Management Plan process?
    A) Work performance information
    B) Deliverables
    C) Project management plan updates
    D) No such information flow occurs

27. All of the following are objectives of Control Communications process EXCEPT:
    A) Optimal information flow occurs
    B) Information needs of project stakeholders are met
    C) Identification of new stakeholders
    D) Trigger a review of Communication Management plan if needed due to an issue

28. Which of the following is NOT a valid tool for risk identification?
    A) The Delphi Technique
    B) Assumptions analysis
    C) Pareto chart
    D) SWOT analysis

29. Which of the following is another name for the fishbone diagram?
    A) Flow chart
    B) Ishikawa diagram
    C) Histogram
    D) Pareto chart

30. Which of the following is an input to Manage Stakeholder Engagement process?
    A) Issue log
    B) Change log
    C) Change request
    D) Work performance data

31. How will you calculate Late Start date and Late Finish date of an activity which has not started yet?
    A) Calculate with backward pass
    B) Calculate with Critical Chain method
    C) Calculate with forward pass
    D) Calculate with Monte Carlo simulation

32. A large project may be subdivided into multiple phases in which process group:
    A) Directing
    B) Planning
    C) Initiating
    D) Executing

33. ____________ is NOT an input to the Develop Project Management Plan process.
    A) Expert judgment
    B) Organizational process assets
    C) Enterprise environmental factors
    D) Project charter

34. You are the project manager of supply chain project. The project has a To Complete Performance Index (TCPI) of 1.1. What does this mean?
    A) Schedule performance needs to be improved more than the cost performance
    B) The project has extra funds at hand
    C) Cost performance needs to be improved more than the schedule performance
    D) Cost performance need to be improved

35. ___________ can be a constraint on the project communication.
    A) Global project with team members in different continents
    B) Schedule, cost, and scope
    C) Stakeholder identification
    D) Sponsor's reporting requirements

36. What would not usually be a manifestation of unique organizational cultures and styles?
    A) Risk taking in decision making
    B) Common beliefs and performance expectations
    C) Organizational policies
    D) Management style of various managers

37. You are working as a project coordinator in an organization and having problems with securing resources for a project. Your manager has turn down each of your request explaining that the resources are already engaged in other work and do not have time to engage with your project. You are working in ___________ organization.
    A) Strong matrix
    B) Functional
    C) Projectized
    D) Weak matrix

38. You are managing a high rise building construction project. The project started six months ago and is now in the middle of executing process group. The team consists of 40 internal resources and 3 sellers. Which of the following reports would be MOST helpful to understand what the status of the project is?
    A) Forecast
    B) Status report
    C) Work performance data
    D) Progress report

39. Which conflict resolution techniques are generally acknowledged and used in project management?
    A) Compromising, accommodating, collaborating, and forcing
    B) Compromising, schmoozing, flattering, and ignoring
    C) Withdrawing, problem solving, ignoring, and compromising
    D) Ignoring, accepting, rejecting, and modifying

40. All of the following are examples of operational work EXCEPT:
    A) Daily newsletter email sent out with important notices
    B) Upgrade of enterprise payroll application every two to three years
    C) Yearly employee performance reviews
    D) Processing of invoices through accounts payable system every two to three days

41. How would you determine the risk rating of a project risk?
    A) Use expert judgment
    B) Multiply probability of occurrence with impact
    C) Use Delphi technique
    D) Adding probability of occurrence and impact

42. If you are working on a global project with resources from multiple countries, which of the following factors will you and your team NOT

consider?
A) Language proficiency
B) Time-zone differences
C) Staff compensation
D) Local holidays

43. A risk audit has various objectives. Which of the following is NOT one of them?
A) Check occurred risks and their root causes
B) Evaluate level of risk management effort in the project
C) Check if any identified risk was missed when planning risk responses
D) Determine if valid risk response planning and follow up was done

44. Formal acceptance of deliverables by the customer at the end of a project phase compared to the end of the project is called ________.
A) Scope validation
B) Earned value management
C) Quality verification
D) Phase gate

45. If Actual Cost is more than the Earned Value, the project is _______.
A) Ahead of schedule
B) Under budget
C) Behind schedule
D) Over budget

46. As project manager you were talking to a team member and discussing how he should approach a certain task. From his body language, you were certain that he does not agree with your approach though he did not refuse. Which of the following BEST represents this situation?
A) Acknowledgement
B) Transmission
C) Distribution
D) Negotiation

47. You are managing a new laptop deployment to the whole workforce of a multi-national company. The company has presence in 45 countries with a global workforce of 65,000. The total number of laptops to be deployed is 31,000. You have team members in each work location to perform the deployment. For each deployment, there is a specific process to set up the user account and several smaller issues need to

be taken care of before the deployment is complete. What can you implement to ensure a quality deployment is done globally?

A) Quality management plan
B) Quality checklist
C) The WBS dictionary
D) Work breakdown structure

48. There is a 70% chance that the material delivery will be late by two days. It is also known that a two day late delivery will result in 10% schedule delay. What is the value of risk?

A) 0.07
B) 0.70
C) Cannot be determined
D) 0.10

49. It is your dream to work on a space exploration project. Currently you are managing an internal system upgrade project for your company. You found out that your company has been awarded a large contract worth several million dollars. This project is part of next generation spaceship development program. What will be your line of action?

A) Fast track your project so that you get a chance to be assigned to the new project
B) Initiate the new project with a project charter
C) Find out how the new project will impact your project
D) Level resources on your project to minimize the impact

50. At what stage, stakeholders have the MOST impact on the project?

A) At project end
B) During execution
C) Throughout project life cycle
D) At project start

51. When a project needs to engage a seller to do part of the work, a statement of work is usually prepared. Which of the following statements do not seem CORRECT about the statement of work?

A) The seller should be able to determine if they can deliver the work from the statement of work
B) It includes desired results, deliverable specifications, and quantity to be delivered
C) Just like the contract, SOW can be modified through contract change control system
D) It is a high level, brief document that helps in negotiations and modifications during contract administration

52. Risk ranking is an output of ___________.
    A) Plan Risk Response process
    B) Expert judgment
    C) SWOT analysis
    D) Qualitative Risk Analysis process

53. You are the project manager of a business application enhancement project. During planning you have identified that internal resources will not be available to perform some work so you have to contract out the work to a seller. You asked the internal resources to provide an estimate of the work. The estimate they provided was $150,000. You went through the procurement process by inviting bids, 30 prospective sellers obtained the statement of work and terms of the contract to review, 24 attended the bidders' conference, but only one submitted bid for $300,000. All of the following may have been the reasons EXCEPT:
    A) Bids were colluded in favor of the submitted bid
    B) SOW was vague and not detailed enough to provide prospective sellers the opportunity to assess their capability to deliver the work
    C) The internal team estimate must be incorrect
    D) The terms of the contract were unfavorable for the seller

54. Which of the following represents verifiable products, services or results?
    A) Change requests
    B) Work breakdown structure components
    C) Deliverables
    D) Project scope statements

55. A public utility project to deploy a new garbage collection policy needed a flyer to be distributed to 100,000 households of the city. A team was developed who went door-to-door to distribute the flyer. In order to verify the flyer is delivered to all the households in the city, few random calls were placed to the residents to find out if they have received the flyer. The tool used to verify quality is known as:
    A) Statistical sampling
    B) Expert judgment
    C) Benchmarking
    D) Validate Scope

56. One of the following tools and techniques is common to all Project

Integration Management processes. Which one is it?
   A) Enterprise environmental factors
   B) Project management information system
   C) Expert judgment
   D) Organizational process assets

57. Which of the following is INCORRECT about the project scope statement?
   A) It provides what work is needed to complete deliverables
   B) It contains work packages
   C) It provides project acceptance criteria
   D) It contains deliverables list

58. You work at a fast paced product development company. One of the requirements set out by the project management office at your company is that each project should create a lessons learned document. Which of the following is the BEST use of lessons learned?
   A) Project performance marketing
   B) Historical data available for future projects
   C) Satisfy project management office requirement
   D) Planning data for this project

59. A project manager asks for every detail from the team members. He meets team members in a daily meeting and gets the details of progress and issues, and provides direction of what steps should be taken to fix an issue. He also reviews every document that is created by the project. He even wants to know if someone wants to go for a coffee break. Which of the following theories fit his management style?
   A) Theory Z
   B) Theory X
   C) Maslow's Theory
   D) Theory Y

60. In which risk management process will you identify Workaround?
   A) Perform Risk Responses
   B) Identify Risks
   C) Plan Risk Responses
   D) Control Risks

61. A new scheduling guideline has been developed by the project management office at your company. The document provides several pieces of information about using resource leveling. Which one of the following it will not have mentioned?

A) It helps with constant resource usage
B) It can change the schedule critical path
C) It removes resource over-allocation
D) It reduces the impact of low skill level of resource

62. A change submitted by a stakeholder was asking for addition of scope that would add significant cost to the project. Which of the following is the MOST likely output of Control Scope process in this case?
A) Rejection letter to the stakeholder who suggested change
B) A change request to add extra cost to budget
C) Update organizational process assets
D) A change request to update performance baselines

63. In which process will you use a qualified sellers list?
A) Conduct Procurements
B) Plan Procurement Management
C) Contract Negotiation
D) Resource Procurements

64. Which of the following is NOT a tool used for managing communications?
A) Work performance reports
B) Communication methods
C) Communication models
D) Performance reporting

65. A senior project manager is trying to explain the goals and objectives of portfolio management to junior project managers at her organization. Which one of the following would she mention as a goal of portfolio management?
A) Provide resources to projects
B) Train, coach, and evaluate project managers
C) Evaluate program and project proposal to derive maximum value out of investment
D) Provide centralized project control activities

66. Two team members were in disagreement over a design issue. One team member had been doing same kind of work over 15 years and was considered an expert in the field while the other team member had only one year experience. The project manager was under pressure to complete a report on the project status that he needed to present to executives so he could not spare much time to resolve this issue. He made the decision based on what the expert resource was saying. What

type of problem solving was this?
A) Forcing
B) Problem solving
C) Withdrawal
D) Compromising

67. A market demand, a business need, or legal requirement commonly results in which of the following?
A) Engaging a stakeholder
B) Hiring a project manager
C) Resourcing a project
D) Initiating a project

68. Which of the following is NOT a characteristic of a decision tree?
A) Assist in identifying hidden risks
B) Shows relative impact of choosing one decision over another
C) Uses the concept of expected monetary value
D) Helps make the most appropriate decision

69. Key stakeholders usually get deeply involved in the project providing help to make the project a success. One stakeholder takes on the responsibility to authorize closure of a project or phase. Who is this stakeholder?
A) Project sponsor
B) Project manager
C) Project management office
D) Key user

70. You are the project manager for a turbine installation project. During the development of work breakdown structure, a team member starts talking about estimating durations of various activities. Your response was that:
A) We should be estimating durations of activities now.
B) If the team decides that they are ready for duration estimation then we should go ahead with it
C) Durations can be estimated only after WBS is done and activities have been defined and sequenced
D) Durations cannot be estimated until cost estimation has been completed

71. There are two kinds of managers in an organization. One type is called manager and the other project leader. Which of the following human resources document will be the BEST to understand the two types of

roles?

A) Reporting structure
B) Job description
C) Fiscal responsibility and number of people reporting
D) Roles and responsibilities

72. Which of the following takes the MOST time on a project?

A) Planning
B) Controlling
C) Executing
D) Designing

73. A new project manager was unsure which technique she should use to come up with a cost estimate for her project. She reviewed the company's estimation guidelines and decided that parametric estimating is the best choice. Which of the following did she use?

A) $300 per day for expert resource
B) Lessons learned from a previous project
C) Project cost distributed down to each activity
D) Project cost summed up from each activity's estimate

74. Which of the following is NOT a tool of the Control Schedule process?

A) Fast tracking
B) Pareto chart
C) Modeling techniques
D) Leads and lags

75. If you receive a complaint from a stakeholder that she is not getting enough information, what will you do?

A) Review stakeholder's information needs and update communication management plan if needed
B) Inform the stakeholder that you have been sending information as per communication management plan
C) Review stakeholder's information needs and send the communication management plan for review
D) Ask the stakeholder to review all project documentation in the project repository

76. As project manager of a payroll application upgrade project, you have to report the project status on a monthly basis to the steering committee. While presenting last month's status you informed the steering committee that the Schedule Performance Index is 1.06 and

the Schedule Variance is $10,000. A steering committee member who is attending this meeting the first time is confused. She represents the finance department so her question is "What does this tell me as to how much we have saved or overspent till now?" What will you tell her based on the information given above?

A) We cannot determine that from this information
B) We have under spent $10,000
C) Earned Value Management is the best technique to see what is the value of the work done and it is presented using indices and variances
D) We have over spent $10,000

77. Which of the following should a project manager use in order to report on the actual project results vs. planned results?
    A) Budget status report
    B) Schedule status report
    C) Variance report
    D) Forecast report

78. Which of the following is NOT an update to the risk register as an output of the Control Risks process?
    A) New identified risks
    B) Risk breakdown structure
    C) Risk response plan
    D) Risk audit results

79. Stakeholder analysis involves all of the following steps EXCEPT:
    A) Identify potential impact each stakeholder can generate
    B) Identify all potential project stakeholders
    C) Classify stakeholders to define an approach strategy
    D) Analyze communication requirements of stakeholders

80. All of the following activities occur in closing process group EXCEPT:
    A) Recording the impacts of process tailoring on the project
    B) Documenting lessons learned
    C) Updating organizational process assets
    D) Recommending corrective actions to fix rejected final deliverable

81. ____________ is an output of Scope Validation process.
    A) Accepted change request
    B) Formal acceptance
    C) Signed statement of work

D) Work breakdown structure

82. A review is done at the end of a phase in order to authorize the close of a phase of the project and start the next phase. This review can be called all of these EXCEPT:
    A) Kill point
    B) Gate review
    C) Phase exit
    D) Kill review

83. A document that has a section on business need and cost-benefit analysis is called ____________.
    A) Project charter
    B) Statement of work
    C) Project management plan
    D) Business case

84. You, as the project manager, are recording impacts of tailoring to the processes. Which process group are you in?
    A) Executing
    B) Initiating
    C) Closing
    D) Monitoring and controlling

85. Which of the following is driven by the organization's risk tolerance?
    A) Cost of risks
    B) Risk responses
    C) Expected Monetary Value
    D) Risks identification

86. A project team working on a complex business application enhancement project stumbles on a serious issue. All work pretty much came to a halt since the team has no idea what the root cause is. You anticipate a delay due to this issue but unsure how much. The team has asked for three days to explore the problem and identify the root cause and solution. How will you proceed?
    A) Inform sponsor and other potentially impacted stakeholders that a serious issue has popped up but you will get back to them with details within 3-4 days
    B) Create a change request document
    C) Add the issue to the lessons learned document
    D) Issue a "stop work until further notice" notification

87. A project manager was advised by a senior project manager to use the 80/20 rule. What was he referring to?
    A) Pareto chart
    B) Validate Scope
    C) Fishbone diagram
    D) Histogram

88. One of your team members came to you with a problem. He is having trouble understanding what is being discussed in the meetings. What will be your advice to him?
    A) Face the speaker and maintain eye contact
    B) Stop the person who is speaking and ask questions
    C) Focus on the speech rather than the speaker
    D) Take minutes of meeting to make the best use of time

89. What is risk appetite?
    A) It is the degree of risk someone will be able to withstand
    B) It is the degree of uncertainty someone is willing to accept while anticipating a reward from it
    C) It is the degree of desire of someone to take on risk
    D) It is the measure of loss that can come from taking the risk

90. Which process group comes to mind when you hear this: Develop Project Charter process and the Identify Stakeholder process?
    A) Monitoring and controlling
    B) Initiating
    C) Inviting
    D) Project charter and stakeholder

91. What is typical about culture in organizations?
    A) Only complex culture will influence a project
    B) Organizations in same geography have same culture
    C) The more complex the project the higher the impact of culture
    D) Culture affects portfolio management but not project management

92. Which of the following is true about Project Integration Management?
    A) It helps various processes to interact with each other
    B) It is a knowledge area concerned with system integration of project's product
    C) It formulates the process of requirement management
    D) It integrates knowledge areas into process groups

93. As project manager of accounts payable system improvement project, you are in the Close Project or Phase process of your project. As part of this phase you will review all of the following EXCEPT:
    A) Execution phase documentation
    B) Contracts
    C) Project charter template
    D) Customer acceptance forms

94. Change request is an output of the Validate Scope process. Which of the following is also an output of the same process?
    A) Accepted deliverables
    B) Work performance data
    C) Requirements document
    D) Product analysis

95. Which of the following statements is INCORRECT about progressive elaboration of project scope?
    A) In progressive elaboration, impact of scope creep is reduced by working in steps
    B) Since a project is unique, progressive elaboration keeps the overall scope objectives intact but details flexible
    C) In progressive elaboration, the specifications and acceptance criteria for deliverables is defined as project moves along
    D) In progressive elaboration, the scope for upcoming work is detailed out as project progresses

96. The process in the Project Integration Management knowledge area that provides the actions necessary to define, develop, and manage all subsidiary plans into a project management plan is ____________.
    A) Develop Project Charter
    B) Direct and Control Project Execution
    C) Develop Project Management Plan
    D) Define and Manage Project work

97. A project manager is facing a dilemma of how to meet the schedule deadline. The project is behind schedule but must be completed on the planned completion date. Which of the following cannot be a solution to this problem?
    A) Remove an activity from the critical path
    B) Add more resource and crash the schedule
    C) Do resource leveling
    D) Fast Track the schedule

98. As a project manager on a non-technology project, how will you define the planning process group?
    A) Define non-technology objectives and plan the technological strategy to meet those objectives
    B) Define project objectives and work on the objectives to achieve results
    C) Define project objectives and plan strategy to meet those objectives
    D) Define non-technology objectives to authorize technology plan

99. A project manager is preparing a document that mentions what information will be expected from stakeholders, when it is expected, in which format and to whom that information will be sent. The project manager is preparing:
    A) Stakeholder register
    B) RACI chart
    C) Communication management plan
    D) Performance report

100. Your company is bidding on a multi-million dollars contract to build parts for spaceship. Which one of the following is the MOST risky contract for your company?
    A) Fixed price
    B) Cost plus incentive
    C) Cost plus fixed-fee
    D) Time and material

101. A junior project manager at your organization is confused about quality control (QC) vs. quality assurance (QA). How will you explain the difference between the two?
    A) QC is controlling the quality and QA is accepting the deliverables after that
    B) QA measures seller's performance while QC measures project performance
    C) Audit department performs QA while project management office performs QC
    D) QC measures the quality of project deliverables and QA audits the results of QC and the quality plan

102. In order to close a project, exit criteria must be defined and verified that the criteria has been met. The criteria can vary from one organization to another or even between types of projects within an organization. Where can the project manager go to find these exit

criteria?
A) Project charter
B) Administrative closure procedures
C) Expert judgment
D) Close Project or Phase

103. A _____ can be used to expedite the development of project schedule.
A) Template
B) Constraint
C) Dependency
D) Project charter

104. You are managing a ship building project when the sponsor invites you to an urgent meeting. He is very worried about the quality of the work being performed. Even after you explain that all the testing has shown satisfactory results, he still believes that the end product will not be of quality. What will be your response?
A) Form a quality assurance team to perform quality audit of the project
B) Get help from senior management to remove sponsor's doubts
C) Explain to the sponsor that his worries are unfounded as all quality results have met the criteria
D) Re-perform some of the test to confirm that the original tests were good

105. A project manager was informed by the sponsor that the product from the project must be delivered one month earlier due to sudden change in market demand. Without changing the scope of the project, what technique can the project manager use to reduce the schedule by one month?
A) Variance analysis
B) Schedule compression
C) Monte Carlo simulation
D) What-if scenario analysis

106. __________________allows a project manager to communicate all approved and rejected changes to the stakeholders.
A) Project team members
B) Configuration management system
C) Change control board
D) Project management information system

107. You are working for a private firm and managing a technology project.

The firm's culture distinctly puts employees into two categories: management and staff. Project managers fall somewhat in the middle. The management considers you as staff member while the project team believes you are the management. So the team members are very reserved in your presence because they think you can impact their performance bonus. Which power do the project team thinks you have?

A) Management power
B) Formal power
C) Referent power
D) Coercive power

108. If the customer asks for a major scope change in the middle of the project by speaking to the project manager directly, what should be her response?
   A) Inform customer that you have to ask sponsor if he is willing to consider the change
   B) Refuse and explain that changes are very expensive in the middle and should be done earlier to avoid extra cost
   C) Mention that any change to the scope means there will be additional cost
   D) Ask customer to send you details of the change in writing so that you can review the impact

109. All of the following are correct about project stakeholders EXCEPT:
   A) They may be affected by the project
   B) They always actively support the project
   C) They may influence the project
   D) They usually are involved in the project

110. One of the following relationships is rarely used when building Precedence Diagrams. Which one is it?
   A) Finish-to-Start
   B) Start-to-Start
   C) Start-to-Finish
   D) Finish-to-Finish

111. A project team decides to use six sigma technique to deliver the 10,000 parts order to the manufacturer. How many defected parts is the project team willing to accept?
   A) One
   B) Two hundred
   C) Zero

D) Three

112. _______ is NOT an input to the Direct and Manage Project Work process.
   A) Stakeholder risk tolerances
   B) Approved change requests
   C) Employee training records
   D) Consultants

113. As project manager you kept all the project documentation on your laptop's hard disk. You have planned for the worst risk, hard disk crash, so took weekly backup on a portable drive that you carried in your laptop bag. One day on your way back from office, you stopped to buy a cup of coffee. When you returned to your car, you found the window broken and the laptop bag gone. Both laptop and the portable backup device were lost. You missed to identify theft as a risk. All of the following could have been a response planned for such a risk EXCEPT:
   A) Keep another backup at office
   B) Password secure the laptop and the portable backup device
   C) Keep the bag with you all the time when not in secure area
   D) Hide the bag in the trunk of the car

114. During negotiation on the contract terms for a construction project, the project manager says, "I want to sign this contract with you because I really like you but my manager is quite upset that you are not listening to what he is asking and I am afraid if you do not accept our terms I won't be able to stop this contract going to another seller". The project manager is using a negotiation tactic, commonly known as?
   A) Good guy, bad guy
   B) Deadline
   C) Divide and rule
   D) Delay

115. What should be included in the scope management plan of an infrastructure project?
   A) Every piece of information that relates to scope
   B) How to manage and control scope
   C) Scope management plan is another name of requirement traceability matrix
   D) Objectives, requirements, deliverables

116. All of the following are tools and techniques of the Close Procurements process EXCEPT:
    A) Procurement negotiations
    B) Payment systems
    C) Records management system
    D) Procurement audits

117. A stakeholder on a project has asked for a change to the project that has an impact on the project budget. To implement the change, _______________ has to be followed.
    A) Change control board
    B) Change's cost estimate
    C) Cost performance baseline
    D) Monitoring and controlling process group

118. Two events will be mutually exclusive when _______________.
    A) Likelihood of one event occurring is higher than the other
    B) They are not impacted by outside factors at the same time
    C) They both cannot happen in a single occurrence
    D) They result in only two succeeding events

119. Considering several feasibility studies are undertaken by organizations every year, which of the following CANNOT be considered a feasibility study?
    A) First phase of a project
    B) A single project
    C) A single program
    D) A pre-project analysis

120. A contract becomes legally binding when both parties have signed and accepted that contract. In which of the following case the contract will not be legally binding even though both parties signed it?
    A) The contract has terms that is in violation of a law
    B) Seller does not perform the work as per contract
    C) It is unacceptable to the legal counsel of buyer or seller
    D) Buyer is unable to make payments to the seller for completed work

121. A project manager has set up a regular weekly project meeting inviting all team members to attend since decisions are to be made. A good discussion on a topic is followed by a decision by the project manager. Any objection by the team member after the decision has been made is considered invalid. Which management style is being used by the

project manager?
  A) Management by objectives
  B) Autocratic
  C) Management by inclusion
  D) Democratic

122. The __________ manager invited three project managers to a meeting to discuss projects' progress. She wants to ensure her role's commitments will be met but has least concern with department's overall strategic goals for the year.
  A) Functional
  B) Program
  C) Project
  D) Portfolio

123. Directing and managing project work process is part of the Executing process group. It is the process of ____________.
  A) Creating project performance report and comparing with the baseline
  B) Creating project charter and identifying stakeholders
  C) Performing the work as per project management plan to achieve project's objectives and goals
  D) Controlling contracts so that the seller performs as per contract

124. Which of the following is not required to have a valid contract?
  A) Seller's contact information
  B) A statement of work or deliverable
  C) Buyer's signatures
  D) Offer and acceptance of the contract

125. You are managing a software development project. Your design team has asked for additional week to complete the design work which is on the critical path. What will you do?
  A) Perform impact assessment of the request
  B) Fast track the schedule to cover up for additional week
  C) Reject the design team's request
  D) Add one week to the project schedule

126. You are excited to start a new project for a highly reputed global company. Even before starting the project, the sponsor has asked for a quick turnaround and wants to move quickly through the initiating and planning process group and get to executing. Which of the following is the MOST effective approach?

A) Use expert judgment to move quickly through initiating and planning
B) Create project charter and move into executing
C) Make active use of progressive elaboration
D) Create project charter, identify risks and stakeholders, and then move to executing

127. Which of the following is NOT a factor that can influence the development of project charter?
A) Infrastructure of the organization
B) Project life cycle
C) Government regulations
D) Marketplace conditions

128. For a new leading edge product development project, the project manager decides to use ________________ to estimate activity durations because there was very little information available about this project.
A) Analogous estimating
B) Guesstimating
C) Parametric estimating
D) Three-point estimating

129. All of the following must be performed during initiation of a project EXCEPT:
A) Divide large projects into phases
B) Identify business needs
C) Evaluate historical information
D) Gather project requirements

130. As project manager, you have provided a unique and verifiable product to your customer and are waiting for her approval. This product has been worked on and prepared by your project team. You are looking forward to start the next phase of your project once you receive customer's approval. What is this unique and verifiable product called?
A) A template
B) A plan
C) A deliverable
D) A project

131. Which of the following estimation techniques results in the most accurate estimate for a new product development project?

A) Analogous estimating
B) Top-down estimating
C) Parametric estimating
D) Bottom-up estimating

132. A project was ahead of schedule with certain hard to achieve deliverables completed earlier than the planned date. The team has been working real hard so the project manager decided to announce an award. Sponsor and other executive stakeholders were invited and two team members were awarded a gift and appreciation certificate. The award ceremony was followed by dinner attended by whole project team along with the executives. Starting next week, project progress started to slow down to the point that next three deliverables were late. What is the BEST step project manager can take?
A) Hold a meeting with the project team to find out what is going on
B) Review the reward system for the project
C) Use problem solving technique with the team members
D) Improve the schedule performance of the project

133. What approach should be taken by the project manager who finds out that the project she is managing requires more time to complete than what has been advised by the customer?
A) Plan to have the resources work overtime to meet the deadline
B) Cut scope to remove activities from the schedule
C) Check if schedule can be compressed to bring the project in time
D) Inform customer that their imposed deadline cannot be met

134. You are the project manager for a non-profit housing project. You had worked with most of the stakeholders before. One of the stakeholders had made quite a few changes on the last project. Which of the following is the BEST approach to manage this stakeholder?
A) Check if this stakeholder can be removed from stakeholders list
B) Set the expectations up right at the start without identifying the stakeholder that too many changes will not be entertained as it is detrimental to the project progress
C) Discuss with stakeholder in an informal verbal way the issue of too many changes
D) Involve the stakeholder actively right from the start of the project

135. A project has a budget of $700,000 and is expected to complete in two years. The project is now 20 percent complete and is on track. What is

the Budget at Completion (BAC)?
   A) $70,000
   B) $700,000
   C) Cannot be determined from the information given
   D) $140,000

136. You are the project manager for a software development project. The code written by the programmers was tested by the testers. Some of the work was found to have significant logical errors that required a complete rewrite. The cost of redoing the work can also be called as:
   A) Cost of non-conformance
   B) Cost of quality
   C) Cost of conformance
   D) Cost of project

137. The project performance can be presented with two indicators that reflect the cost and schedule performance of the project. These are:
   A) Cost Planning Index (CPI) and Schedule Performing Index (SPI)
   B) Cost Planned Index (CPI) and Schedule Planned Index (SPI)
   C) Cost Performance Index (CPI) and Schedule Performance Index (SPI)
   D) Cost Variance (CV) and Earned Value (EV)

138. As project manager, you created and received approval of the project charter for your project. The charter has formally authorized you to start project work. It includes high level requirements, assumptions, and constraints. How often are you planning to review the project charter?
   A) Never
   B) Every time I meet the sponsor
   C) Quarterly
   D) Monthly

139. Which of the following is included in a project charter?
   A) Resource requirement for each WBS work package
   B) Project communication plan
   C) The business need for the project
   D) Cost estimate for each WBS work package

140. A programmer working on a global project repeatedly produced code with errors that required significant rework to fix. This is an issue of resource___________.
   A) Competency

B) Programming
C) Authority
D) Allocation

141. You are managing a global software development project. There are several teams located in different countries. One of the teams is continuously late in producing its deliverables which is affecting another team's schedule. What will be your approach to fix this problem?
A) Bring both team leaders in a meeting and discuss the issue
B) Discuss issue with the leader of the team that receives the late deliverables
C) No need to take action as second team is still able to produce their deliverables on time somehow
D) Discuss issue with the leader of the team that produces the late deliverables

142. The project manager is reconciling the expense plan with any funding limits imposed by the approved budget. What process is this?
A) Determine Budget
B) Integrated Change Control
C) Control Costs
D) Estimate Costs

143. You were the project manager of project X which was a finance application upgrade project and was completed successfully a year ago. Since then you have moved on to a different role in the human resources department. Project Y, which is a follow up project to project X, is in its initiation process. The project manager of project Y has identified you as a stakeholder of the project. How should she classify you?
A) High power, high influence
B) High power, high interest
C) Low influence, high impact
D) Low power, high influence

144. Which process takes into account resource usage data, resource productivity, and budget and schedule variances?
A) Control Schedule
B) Project Human Resources Management
C) Work Performance Data
D) Monitor and Control Project Work

145. A project manager has many types of contracts to consider when deciding which will be more suitable for the type of work to be done. Which one of the following is NOT a type of contract?
   A) Cost plus fixed-fee
   B) Statement of work
   C) Time and material
   D) Fixed-price

146. What is the duration of the critical path in this activity list?

Activity	Duration	Predecessor
A1	2	
A2	3	A1
A3	4	A1
B1	5	A2
B2	6	A3
B3	7	A3
C1	4	B2
C2	3	B3
D1	4	B1
D2	2	C1,C2
E1	3	D1
E2	4	E1,D2

   A) 20
   B) 22
   C) 24
   D) 21

147. A project manager needs to identify the most important factor that should be considered so that the right project is selected for implementation. This factor is:
   A) Project budget
   B) Business needs
   C) Project scope
   D) Project constraints

148. Which of the following is expected to be within the Initiating Process Group?
   A) Develop Project Charter
   B) Develop Project Management Plan
   C) Collect Requirements

D) Define Scope

149. Cost of nonconformance has all of the following characteristics EXCEPT:
A) Safety measures
B) Loss of customers
C) Rework
D) Liabilities

150. When performing Earned value analysis, you consider all of the following EXCEPT:
A) Budgeted cost of work performed
B) Value of work completed
C) Actual cost of work performed
D) Planned cost of contingency reserve

151. You are managing a large end to end application development project. After completing the requirements gathering phase, the project ended up with 3,000 requirements. Managing those requirements is a huge challenge but you know of a tool that can help your project manage all 3000 requirements along with the attributes. What is this tool called?
A) Configuration management plan
B) Requirements traceability matrix
C) Requirements document
D) Project management plan

152. Which of the following is NOT a characteristic of the payment system?
A) Terms of the contract are not negotiated in the payment system
B) Payment request is reviewed and approved before payment is made
C) Payments to the seller are usually handled by accounts receivable system
D) Payment is made according to the terms of the contract

153. Which of the following is the way to be more effective for a pharmaceutical company researching a new drug, getting approval and marketing it?
A) Portfolio management
B) Program management
C) As an operational activity
D) Separate projects for research, drug approval, and marketing

154. A project manager has been working on a new corporate intranet development project. The work has been going quite smoothly. No budget or schedule overruns have occurred. The designers have created amazing web applications that meet the needs of the customer really well. In the last design review meeting, the lead designer suggested an application that will create real time reports by combining employee personal data, payroll data, and data from learning management system. The team really liked the idea because they felt the report will be a great time saver for any employee looking for the information. Surprisingly the requirements document does not mention any such report so it seems this is out of scope. What should the project manager do?
    A) Speak with the sponsor and inform about this great application that will be very productive
    B) Consult change control process and perform impact assessment
    C) Reject the application idea as it is out of scope. Focus on completing the project and do not entertain such ideas
    D) Include the application into requirement to deliver it with the rest of the intranet and so exceed customer expectations

155. During a team meeting to select a seller after the submitted bids were opened and reviewed, project team members could not decide who to award the contract. One member recommended a seller who is highly reputed in the industry, another member recommended a seller that has worked for the company several times before, yet another member insisted that the seller who has the lowest bid should be awarded the contract. What should the project manager do?
    A) Review the seller selection criteria
    B) Verify seller's reputation in the market
    C) Select the lowest bidder
    D) Contact project managers who have worked with seller before and ask their opinion

156. Which one of the following is the BIGGEST benefit of using a co-located team?
    A) Team communication and collaboration is more effective
    B) Reduces the communication project manager has to do with the team
    C) It costs much less because team members are located in same location
    D) Team communication is no longer required when team members are located in the same location

157. A contract had terms that defined that ten resources will be engaged on the project by the supplier to execute the statement of work. During execution both buyer and seller find that more resources are needed. Therefore, the seller requests that two more resources will be added to the contract. How will the buyer proceed with seller's request?
    A) Buyer will follow the contract change control system to modify the contract
    B) Though both buyer and seller agree that two more resources need to be added, the contract cannot be changed
    C) This is a perfect example of controlling contract where alternative dispute resolution is needed
    D) The buyer will cancel the current contract and sign a new contract by putting number of resources as twelve

158. A warning sign in regards to risk response is also called as ________.
    A) Impact
    B) Risk trigger
    C) Threshold
    D) Probability

159. Which type of communication can the project status report be considered?
    A) Informal written communication
    B) Formal written communication
    C) Informal verbal communication
    D) Formal verbal communication

160. Which of the following is the point where optimal quality is reached?
    A) Revenue from improvements equal the incremental costs to achieve the improvements
    B) The test results just meet the specifications and the product is not of unnecessary high quality
    C) Revenue from corrective actions equals the revenue from defect repair
    D) Results from quality audit are the same as results from quality control measurements

161. A project manager who was already managing a project was assigned a new project. Due to commitments on the other project, she wanted to create the work breakdown structure rather quickly. What will be your advice?
    A) Work breakdown structure can be skipped in favor of a quick

high level activities list, if time is in short supply
B) Only drill down 2-3 levels and create work package at a higher level
C) Ask the sponsor to have the key users prepare work breakdown structure
D) Head start work breakdown structure from a similar previous project as a template

162. You are in the steering committee meeting presenting your project's latest performance report. You just presented that the CPI is 1.1 and the SPI is 0.87. Which of the following is the next logical piece of information you should share?
A) Work completed during reporting period
B) Current status of risks
C) Forecasted project completion
D) Outstanding issues

163. Which of the following statements is incorrect about the Project Management Plan?
A) It contains the cost performance baseline
B) It contains risk management plan
C) It consists of several supplementary plans
D) It identifies the business need of the project plan

164. Which of the following input can help the project manager the MOST when creating a cost estimate for her project?
A) Parametric estimate
B) Work breakdown structure
C) Sponsor's commitment
D) Resource breakdown structure

165. You are looking at the following list of activities (in sequence) for a small software functionality enhancement project. Calculate the minimum time it will take to deploy the project when all the activities are on a critical path and activity 6 is late by 6 days while activity 5 was completed one day earlier?
1) Gather requirements - 3 days
2) Create Specs document - 2 days
3) Design the changes - 3 days
4) Code the changes - 5 days
5) Unit Testing - 6 days
6) Business Testing - 12 days
7) Deployment - 1 day

8) Post deployment support - 10 days

A) 37 days
B) 47 days
C) 32 days
D) 42 days

166. You were managing a project that had a seller work under a cost reimbursable contract. The project has reached the Close Procurements process. What is it that you have to do?
A) Negotiate payment terms
B) Update project management plan
C) Ensure seller resources are taken off project as soon as the work is completed
D) Audit seller's invoices

167. Thinking about project budget requirements, these can be:
A) Incremental and/or lump sum
B) Cost-based or schedule-based
C) Contingency and management reserve
D) Parametric or parabolic estimates

168. What happens in the Perform Quality Assurance process?
A) Quality requirements of the project are audited and the results from quality control measurements are reviewed to verify that the quality standards imposed in the project are adequate and that relevant policies of the organization are followed
B) Audits the submissions by the vendor to ensure the payment requested matches the payment plan
C) Quality measurements are compared against deliverable specifications to ensure the deliverable meets the set criteria
D) Provides the performance level to the project team to be able to audit the project quality measurements

169. Which process area includes vendor selection and documenting lessons learned?
A) Direct and Manage Project Work
B) Project Procurement Management
C) Project Scope Management
D) Close Project or Phase

170. CMMI is a technique that is used for:
A) Ensuring that CPI and SPI do not fall below 1.0
B) Creating project budget with the help of experts

C) Performing quality audit of projects
D) Measuring and controlling project quality

171. Which of the following process groups must occur at least once in all projects?
A) Planning, executing, and monitoring and controlling
B) Initiating and closing
C) Initiating, planning, executing, monitoring and controlling, and closing
D) Initiating, planning, and closing

172. All of the following are always characteristics of a project EXCEPT:
A) Specific outcome
B) Temporary
C) Progressively elaborated
D) Strategic

173. A project manager was having problems with issues popping up without any warning. The project team is regularly doing risk identification, analysis and response planning. What could have gone wrong?
A) Project team is less experienced
B) Project team is doing lip service only
C) Project team needs training in issue management
D) Project team is creating poor risk responses

174. Which of the following will you consider for the staff management plan?
A) Communication strategy
B) Organizational Theory
C) Position Descriptions
D) Safety

175. Each of the following can be present in a project EXCEPT:
A) Only one resource working on the project
B) Project ends without producing a deliverable
C) Project deliverable is not specified
D) Project stakeholders not impacted by the project after it ends

176. The QA team performed __________ to verify if the gain from improving quality is equal to or lower than the incremental cost to achieve that quality.
A) Monte Carlo simulation

B) Just in time
C) Marginal analysis
D) Kaizen event

177. What can a project manager do to resolve a dispute with a seller? The dispute is over scope change where the seller believes that the scope is extra work and not part of the signed contract while the buyer believes it is already included in the contract.
A) Contract can be terminated
B) If seller does not agree then the buyer can go to the court
C) Contract can be changed to resolve the dispute
D) Alternative dispute resolution technique can be used

178. A project manager working for a chemical equipment manufacturing company has been working on a long project. The project has finally reached completion and is in the Close Project process. The project manager has requested customer to provide formal acceptance of the new chemical mixing machine. All of the following statements are normally true in regards to the final acceptance of the new machine EXCEPT:
A) The customer should use the machine for one year before confirming that all terms of the contract have been met
B) The customer should conduct performance testing on the new machine
C) The customer can use third party testing to confirm if the machine meets the specifications
D) The customer should confirm in writing that all terms of the contract have been fulfilled

179. The project is officially approved to go ahead when:
A) Deliverables have been accepted
B) Project manager is assigned
C) Project charter is approved
D) Stakeholders are identified

180. A project had identified and analyzed a list of risks and planned responses to few of them. One of the risks occurred and the project manager responded as per plan. The expected monetary value of the risk was $10,000 but the additional cost incurred, due to occurrence of that risk, was $15,000. Still the project manager believed that the outcome was better than expected. Why?
A) Project is still ahead of schedule and under budget
B) Expected Monetary Value is not a cost of the impact

C) Project manager does not understand Expected Monetary Value concept
D) Project was under budget and had extra funds available

181. Several senior managers at a large wholesale distribution company recently got trained in project management. They were very impressed with the structure and rigor of project management processes and decided that all orders received by the company will be considered projects. They even changed the titles of customer representatives to project managers and got them trained on project management fundamentals. Each order will be treated as a project request, a project manager is pre-assigned to projects based on origin of the project, status will be updated daily, issues will be recorded against the project and resolved, and scope validation will occur with customer's acceptance of the shipment. The orders can be anywhere from $10 through internet to $300,000 through EDI purchase order. In order to reduce the burden on project manager, project charter and project management plan have been eliminated. What would be your comments?
A) All the projects are operational activity and should not be treated as projects
B) Any effort that is temporary, has a start and end date and results in a product is a project so the orders are treated correctly as projects
C) Orders that takes more than 5 days to process should be treated as projects and the rest as operational activity
D) Since there is a continuous flow of related projects, it can be considered as a program

182. A project manager at your organization was having trouble controlling the project scope. You advised him to refer to _______ for guidance.
A) Scope management plan
B) Requirements traceability matrix
C) Scope control plan
D) Scope validation plan

183. Which is an interpersonal skill a project manager uses MOST often?
A) Compromising
B) Coaching
C) Influencing
D) Collaborating

184. Benchmarking technique results in one or all of the following

EXCEPT:

A) Provide a basis for measuring performance
B) Identify best practices
C) Measure project performance against the plan
D) Generate ideas for improvement

185. You are the project manager of a financial services project. There is tremendous pressure from stakeholders to shorten the project schedule. You decided to use a schedule compression technique called crashing. You may do any of these activities EXCEPT:

A) Provide incentive to vendor for early delivery of code
B) Engage more resources
C) Get resources to work overtime
D) Reduce the scope of project

186. What is a list of qualified sellers?

A) A list of sellers who have qualified people in their teams
B) A list of sellers whose qualifications and experiences are found to be competent to perform the work
C) A list of sellers whose qualifications and experiences have been reviewed thoroughly
D) A list of sellers whose qualifications and experiences are of highest quality

187. You are the project manager for a dam construction project where major pieces of work have been contracted out to two contractors. You have observed that one of the contractors is not delivering the work as per contract. After reviewing the terms of that contract, you are quite clear that some of the contractual terms were not met by the contractor. You decided to start some corrective action to make sure the contractor performs as stipulated in the statement of work and the contract. All of the following can be an output of your effort EXCEPT:

A) Updating the organizational process assets
B) Work performance data
C) Change request
D) Contractor's performance evaluation

188. You are managing a global application deployment project. Part of the work is to be done on a very specialized software for which it is really hard to find a resource. You were lucky and got a contract resource engaged. In the middle of execution, the resource resigned. What will you do?

A) Distribute the work to other resources
B) Assess the impact of the lost resource on the project
C) Fast Track the schedule
D) Reject the resignation and demand that the resource come back to work and complete the project

189. A project manager left the company for some personal reasons right after he received approval of project charter. You were asked to take over the project. What will be your FIRST step?
A) Redo risk identification
B) Work on gathering detailed requirements
C) Start planning the project
D) Check all stakeholders' alignment with project charter

190. If someone asks you what a program is, what will be your response?
A) A program consists of projects from one department trying to achieve the strategic goals of the department
B) A program is a set of projects running concurrently
C) A program is a result of government mandate to comply with legislation
D) A program is a way to meet business needs by coordinating and controlling multiple related projects

191. Which one of the following will you NOT consider when planning the communication needs of a project?
A) Geographical location of resources
B) Number of resources
C) Project duration
D) Experience as project manager

192. An application enhancement project is being executed and has reached the end of design phase 10 days earlier than planned and 20% under the planned expense. Next the development phase is to start, followed by multiple testing iterations. Design team and development team are not co-located. What is the FIRST thing project manager will do?
A) Team building
B) Validate scope
C) Hire additional developers
D) Control quality

193. What can be done if a large complex project, engaging several hundred resources, is cancelled in the middle of execution?
A) Update lessons learned document and perform the administrative

closure

B) Convince management to take back their decision as several hundred families get affected by their decision

C) Work with other projects and programs to transfer resources

D) Identify upcoming projects and explore opportunity for yourself and your team

194. What is true about analogous estimating?

A) It is more accurate than bottom-up estimating

B) It is very rarely used

C) It is less accurate than bottom-up estimating

D) It is as same accurate as bottom-up estimating

195. A project manager was informed by the team member that the internal failure cost is very high. Which of the following is an example of internal failure cost that the team member may be referring to?

A) Liabilities

B) Rework

C) Destructive testing

D) Quality control

196. Why are Enterprise Environmental Factors an input to the Direct and Manage Project Work process?

A) Enterprise Environmental Factors are an input to Develop Project Management Plan and not to Direct and Manage Project Work

B) Enterprise Environmental Factors provide standard guidelines and work instructions

C) Enterprise Environmental Factors include project management information system which provides the tools for executing the project

D) Enterprise Environmental Factors are needed to get the change request approved

197. You are managing a software development project. Why should you include the project team members to contribute to the lessons-learned document?

A) To show the sponsor that team has done a good job

B) Project Close process requires that project team members be included as part of this exercise

C) To help teams working on projects in future be successful

D) To give the team a feeling of accomplishment and/or vent their frustration

198. Which of the following is an INCORRECT statement about the configuration management system?
    A) It is part of the project management information system
    B) It is a part of the change management system
    C) It defines how changes will be controlled
    D) It identifies change submission and tracking process

199. All of the following statements are correct about a bidders' conference EXCEPT:
    A) A bidders' conference should have ample time so that all the sellers have a chance to ask questions
    B) Answer to a seller's question should be openly provided to all the sellers
    C) Objective is to have all sellers develop a same understanding of the bid
    D) First time bidders should be given extra attention to encourage them to bid

200. All of the following statements about critical chain method are incorrect EXCEPT:
    A) Critical chain method is also critical path method
    B) Critical chain method creates an effective schedule when resources are abundant
    C) Critical chain method uses mandatory dependencies exclusively
    D) Critical chain method creates an effective schedule when resources are limited

5 - ANSWERS & EXPLANATIONS TEST 1

1: A

New risks that are identified throughout project life cycle are analyzed, risk triggers are monitored, and contingency reserve is analyzed in the Control Risks process. Risk mitigation strategy is developed in Plan Risk Response process.

2: B

The Actual Cost (AC) for 6 month of work = $720,000 while the Planned Value (PV) for the same period is $600,000. There is no Earned Value (EV) information given. In order to find out schedule (SV) and cost variances (CV), EV is required. Hence, there is not enough information to determine how the project is doing.

3: A

Work performance reports is the input to the Manage Project Team process. It is created from work performance information which is generated from work information data. There is no such thing as work performance standards in this context.

4: D

The organization must have a high cost of quality. Remember that cost of quality includes cost of conformance and non-conformance both. So significant effort and money is being spent to achieve a high quality. Low cost of quality will result in low quality so this is incorrect choice. Project schedule's robustness does not impact the quality as such. Using a standard quality management plan alone cannot guarantee quality. It is what is in the plan that counts more than whether a standard plan is used or not.

5: B

Control Costs process can only work once a cost baseline has been established otherwise there is nothing against which costs can be controlled.

6: B

Expert judgment is not an input; it is a tool and technique used to develop project charter. The other three are input to the Develop Project Charter process.

7: A

The defined processes of the organization including policies and procedures fall under enterprise environmental factors. The question is asking about the process not the approval requirement, so government requirement is a wrong choice.

8: A

It is a detailed description of deliverables to be produced by the project. Terms and conditions (T&C) of the contract are separate from the statement of work (SOW). T&C provide how the work defined in the SOW is to be performed. Project charter defines work at a very high summary level. The project scope statement is also a high level description of work compared to the statement of work.

9: B

In a weak matrix organization, the functional manager has much direct responsibility of the project than in most other types of organizations. The project manager role is more that of an expediter, and hence depends on decision making by the functional manager. Therefore, a project manager cannot be the only one held responsible for the project.

10: B

Final deliverable is not an organizational process asset; it is the product of the project and is validated in Monitor and Control Project Work. Project files which are the documents created by the project, historical information that includes lessons learned, and formal acceptance forms all get added to the organizational process assets therefore these are the updates.

11: C

The controlling process in Project Stakeholder Management is called Control Stakeholder Engagement.

12: C

"If I do not get the document from you within two days, I will speak with your manager." The project manager is using coercive power to get the work done. Complaint to the manager may bring the issue of resource's performance and will be damaging for the resource. "I want you to complete this report by end of tomorrow." This statement can only be made where there is formal power in play. "Should I meet in person or just send her an email. Which is the right approach?" Here the project manager is relying on expert judgment of the resource. "Come on. You know you owe me. Get me the report tomorrow." This is an example of use of referent power by the project manager.

13: C

Risk response is not a type of risk attitude shown by organizations. It is the result of showing an attitude represented by the other three choices.

14: B

Your biggest concern should be scope creep since the applications provide different functionalities and there is a big possibility that the focus may shift from delivering customer requirements to bringing in cool functionality. Budget, schedule and quality are not of concern at this time because no such information has been given in the question.

15: C

Closing processes should not be skipped for any kind of project. This process is an essential part of project management to confirm that the project has delivered what it was required to deliver, stakeholders' needs have been met, etc.

16: B

A root cause analysis should be done to find why the customer is still dissatisfied. Verifying quality measurements alone does not provide the reasons of continued customer dissatisfaction. Identifying how many survey results are outside limits only tells the severity of dissatisfaction and not the reasons. Pareto chart can be built only once the reasons for dissatisfaction are found out. Root cause analysis can help with that.

17: C

The schedule management plan will provide the guideline and criteria to create and manage project schedule. Schedule baseline is the end result of creating schedule. Resource management plan is about managing resources not schedule. There is no such plan as activity management plan.

18: C

Lessons learned mostly benefit the future project and not necessarily the project where these are produced. Work performance data is about measuring the progress of work and mostly contains the information. It does not provide any corrective or preventive action. Issue log records only information and result related to issues and does not encompass every aspect of the project. Project management plan is updated based on information and results from all sources. For example, work performance information, issue log, lessons learned, all provide results which when incorporated in project management plan benefits the project the MOST.

19: A

Though all four skills are used by the project manager, public speaking will be the least effective one to be used for coordinating toward accomplishing a goal. So this is the correct choice.

20: D

You are referring to a qualified sellers' list. This is a shortlist of all sellers who have the capability to perform the work. So by only inviting those sellers, you save time going through the Conduct Procurement process. Negotiating a contract happens when a seller has been selected. Evaluation criteria is established before a list of firms is to be created based on that criteria. Solicitation packages will be sent out after the list is available.

21: B

Human resources are engaged in the Acquire Project Team process during project execution. In Develop Project Team process, the engaged resources start working together as a team. In storming, project team starts to address the project work as well as the approach to manage the project. There is no such process as engage resources.

22: B

Negotiation is the quickest and cheapest method of conflict resolution followed by mediation which involves engaging a 3rd party to help come to an agreement. If this fails then arbitration is where an arbitrator is appointed and agreed to by both the parties and the decision of the arbitrator is binding. It takes much more time but still is settled outside the court. The most expensive and time taking technique is through litigation. Escalation and confirmation are not the techniques for dispute resolution.

23: D

Manage Stakeholder Engagement does not involve tracking team member's performance. Neither Monitoring and Controlling nor Develop Project Team processes track performance or provide feedback to the team member. Manage Project Team is the execution process where team member performance is tracked and feedback is provided.

24: B

Since budget baseline is a part of the planned project performance it is a weak choice. Completion of planned work as per project management plan happens in Direct and Manage Project Work process. Actual project performance is compared with the baselines not just cost performance baseline in the Monitor and Control Project Work.

25: B

Apparently it seems that project C comes after project B which comes after project A but without further information about the projects this may not be true. The three projects may start at the same time or staggered or overlapped. The work qualifies as project work since it has a definite start and end, will result in a unique product, and will go through progressive elaboration: Therefore it cannot be considered as operational work. This is more of a project with three phases than a program because the deliverables out of each phase and overall project are well defined and clear.

26: D

Schedule Performance Index = Earned Value / Planned Value
SPI = 0.8 = EV / 150,000
Solving for EV, EV = $120,000
Schedule Variance = EV - PV = $120,000 - $150,000 = -$30,000

27: A

Management's mandate results in more strategic projects being initiated. Improvement in project management practice has the least impact on taking on strategic projects. Resources are managed by project managers not project management office. Training sessions may improve project managers' capability to manage resources but does not transfer the responsibility from one to another. Stage gate reviews have to be scheduled whether project manager's performance has improved or not. The results have no impact on this. Since training, coaching and mentoring is one of the functions of the project management office, these results confirm that PMO has been able to deliver on one of their functions. This is a result that should please the PMO manager.

28: D

Selecting appropriate processes for the project is always the responsibility of the project manager. Prioritizing projects based on business need is usually done by the portfolio management team. Writing performance reports for project resources is mostly done by functional managers. Meeting the project's profit margin is only valid when working for an external customer.

29: C

Overcoming resistance to change and building trust are the examples of interpersonal skills so this is the right answer. Since writing and negotiation are management skills, the other three choices are wrong.

30: D

The main objective of assigning a project manager to a project is to increase the probability of achieving project goals. So a project manager, who has been assigned to an in-trouble project, will focus on factors and issues that have the biggest impact on meeting project objectives. The question does not specify schedule delay being an issue so this is too narrow an answer and cannot be the best choice. Control procurements only happens when a seller is engaged to do some work. The question does not provide any such information so this is also not the right choice. Communication improvement can definitely help a project in trouble but since the question does not specify that there is a communication issue, this cannot be selected as the right answer especially in the presence of a better choice.

31: D

Project risk acceptance is just one of the strategies and may be best in certain circumstances but definitely not all. Risk identification whether positive or negative is just one step: identified risks also need to be analyzed, response planned and then implemented. To make risk management effective, risks should be tracked even after they have occurred so that the response strategy is modified to manage these successfully.

32: C

Manage Communications and Manage Stakeholder Engagement are part of the executing process group. Plan Communications Management is part of planning process group. Only Control Communications is part of the monitoring and controlling process group.

33: C

Completing project on time and within budget does not always satisfy project stakeholders. Stakeholders' satisfaction requires their needs being met through completed deliverables and their perception that they have received the best value from the project. Projects do have an impact on future projects in the organization at least through lessons learned. A project can succeed without a project manager being formally assigned to the project. Progressive elaboration is needed as project progresses so that effective plans are in place.

34: B

Controlling quality identifies the ways to eliminate causes of unsatisfactory performance because results are compared against the standards and defects are identified in this process. This provides the direction as to how the unsatisfactory performance can be corrected. There is no process called perform quality performance. Project Quality Management is the knowledge area and not a process. Perform Quality Assurance checks the adequacy of project quality management as well as compliance with organizational policies.

35: D

This is work performance data that can be analyzed using earned value technique. Quality audits are usually performed by 3rd party but in any case a formal report is produced after the audit. Time and cost estimating happens during planning process and does not include measurements from quality tests or how much work has been completed.

36: D

The bidders' conference is held in the Conduct Procurements process which includes inviting sellers to bid for the work and awarding the contract. Plan Procurement Management happens before bids are invited and Control Procurements happens after bid has been awarded. Close Procurements happen after the work has been completed.

37: A

Acquire Project Team, Develop Project Team and Manage Project Team processes fall under the Executing process group and therefore are part of Direct and Manage Project Work process. Acquire Project Team and Manage Project Team are the processes mentioned in the question so these cannot be the answer. Monitor and Control Project Work is an incorrect choice.

38: C

Project management plan and risk register are the ones that get updated during Close Project or Phase process. Expert judgment is not an organizational process asset; it is a tool and technique. Project charter and business case are not updated unless the project objectives have significantly changed. This, of course, cannot happen in Close Project or Phase process.

39: C

At any point during project initiation, planning and execution, whether the project is 50% or more complete or not, once a new stakeholder has been identified, stakeholder register and stakeholder management strategy should be updated. All the other three options are incorrect.

40: C

Parametric estimation technique uses historical data and statistical analysis to come up with project cost estimate. In bottom-up estimating, estimates at activity level are made and then summed up to the project level. Analogous estimating is a high level estimating technique that does take historical information into account but does not uses any statistical analysis. There is no such technique called as risk based estimating.

41: C

Managing project resources and assigning project tasks is the responsibility of the project manager and is not taken care of by the project management office. All the other three are responsibilities of the project management office.

42: A

Since additional resources are available that can be engaged by the project, you should crash the schedule. Fast tracking would be running activities in parallel. This increases risk compared to crashing the schedule. Resource leveling usually results in extending the schedule. Estimating activity resources is irrelevant in this case.

43: C

The purpose of the quality assurance process is to review quality management plan, quality measurements, and compliance against company's quality policies and procedures. Most information for lessons learned will come out of this process. Identify stakeholders is mainly an initiating process, while Plan Quality Management and Plan Communications Management are planning processes and are focused on planning and using lessons learned and other artifacts from previous projects.

44: B

Project management office is an organization so this cannot be the correct answer. Integrated change control system is to manage change requests not schedules, so this is incorrect. Organizational process assets include processes, procedures and knowledge base so this is also not the right choice. Enterprise environmental factors include organization's infrastructure. Since desktop scheduling software falls under infrastructure, this is the best answer.

45: A

PERT analysis is a technique used for time estimation not for schedule control. All other three are Control Schedule process tools and techniques. Resource leveling is a resource optimization technique while What-If scenario analysis is a Modeling technique.

46: C

Understanding where the non-value added work is happening and what are the limitations being faced is done through process analysis. Quality assurance or quality audit does not uncover non-value added work or limitations being faced, it verifies if the company policies and procedures are being followed. Scatter diagram compares two factors against each other and does not address the issues in question.

47: C

Verifying that project results comply with relevant quality standards is part of the Control Quality process and not a part of quality assurance process. Therefore, this is the right choice.

48: D

Tracking cost both ways requires effort and without the knowledge of how much effort is needed, it is not a prudent step to take. You also cannot just track costs as requested by customer, since you need to provide the data for your company's internal consumption which requires that costs be tracked by resources. A refusal without a valid reason will not be acceptable by the customer. So you should evaluate to find out the cost of complying with customer's demand. This will provide you the knowledge to make further decision and/or communication.

49: D

A business case, project requirements document, and project scope statement do not include a summary milestone schedule. Only project charter has it so this is the right choice.

50: D

Milestones are not required to build a schedule though they are strongly recommended. Activities cannot be summed up in milestones since milestones have zero duration and zero cost associated with them. WBS work packages cannot be called milestones but chunks of work to produce deliverables. Milestones can be a requirement of sponsor so that he/she can see the project's progress in definite terms.

51: B

Since we are looking for biggest impact, without clear roles and responsibilities, a project manager's experience, technical expertise of the team and co-location may not be much effective.

52: B

Expected monetary value, for each option that was evaluated, is the output of decision tree analysis. Expected monetary value is not the cost of managing the risk.

53: B

Estimate At Completion (EAC) is the total expense at the end of the project. Hence, it is the sum of Actual Cost (AC) till now and the Estimate To Complete (ETC) the rest of the project work.

EV and AC will provide Cost Variance (CV) and Cost Performance Index (CPI). CPI and AC will provide EV and hence CV. Same way CPI, AC, and EV provide CV only.

All three wrong choices measure past performance and do not provide any information regarding future.

54: D

The role of project sponsor is to help the project manager resolve issues and be able to achieve project's objectives. Communicating with stakeholders is the responsibility of the project manager and so are, managing integrated change control process and providing project status to management.

55: C

Stakeholders who are affected by the project should be included in the project charter. Executive level stakeholders and stakeholders who will be directly involved in the project work are a subset of the first group. Stakeholders who have an interest in the project but have no influence or are not affected by the project are actually not stakeholders.

56: B

The biggest benefit a project manager gets from stakeholder classification and analysis is that he/she does not have to spend too much time managing their needs. Though it is true that most stakeholders have very limited time to spend on the project, classifying them does not affect the time they have to spend. Assigning responsibilities comes from defining roles and responsibilities, not by putting individual stakeholder into a different group. Classifying stakeholders in a group identifies how they are to be managed. Stakeholders do not need to know which group they belong to. In fact releasing this information to stakeholders can backfire.

57: B

Answering questions of prospective sellers happens during Conduct Procurements process. During Control Procurements process, the contract has already been awarded so there are no more prospective sellers. All other three options are part of Control Procurements process.

58: C

Since the problem has already occurred this has become an issue and is no longer a risk so it should be treated as an issue. This is true but a weak answer. The best way to handle is to evaluate the impact of this issue on performance baselines and proceed further from there. Of course the expectation is that appropriate communication has occurred so that next shipment does not end up on the wrong side. It is of no value to have this added to the risk register, analyzed and response planned since it has already occurred. Contingency reserve is not for unplanned risk, it is setup and used for planned risks.

59: B

Preventive actions reduce the chances of negative outcomes of actions. Activity that can help improve performance back to the desired state is a corrective action. The other two options do not make much sense.

60: B

Noise is something that either distracts the receiver of the information or creates obscurity in the message when it is being received. In other words it interferes with the understanding of the message by the receiver. Noise does not change the message but it impacts understanding of the message. Noise can be persistent or occasional, it can affect both ways. The noise in the question is the one discussed in communication models and not just the physical noise.

61: A

Spelling errors: Both activities mentioned are quality control activities. Nuts counting: Both activities mentioned are quality control activities. Book title printing: Both represent same activity which is a quality control activity. Wheel diameter: Measuring diameter of wheel to see if it is within limits is quality control activity but making sure that the limits set are correct is quality assurance activity. This is the correct choice.

62: B

Events are the result of a known or unknown project risk occurring and these may or may not result in an impact. Conditions resulting from organization's environment contribute to project risks.

63: A

Policy documents are not created from templates because each policy document is different and addresses different areas. That is why it is being created in the first place. Also policy documents are not created within projects but in the organization larger than the project. Resource training procedure is developed by the human resources department and not within a project unless it is a deliverable of a project. A template can be used to create requirements document but not requirement gathering which is a process. Project scope statement can definitely be created from a template. This is the right answer.

64: A

These are constraints on the project. In other words they set boundary for the project. These cannot be called scope of work or deliverables but do provide boundary of when and how work or deliverables are to be completed. These are not assumptions since these are not unknowns being taken as reality.

65: C

If the approach being taken to develop an industry leading product is totally new, the quality plan should be created from scratch and updated with continuous involvement of the stakeholders. Delaying the plan is out of the question since there is nothing to verify that the work being done is of quality. Using an old plan cannot work effectively as the project has a totally new approach even if the old plan was from a successful product development project. Project team's preferred tests may not be the right tests so this option cannot be correct.

66: A

The reason there can be a wide difference between bids is that each prospective seller has a different understanding of the statement of work and terms and conditions. Both of these documents should be evaluated if these are clear enough and provide same understanding of the work to all prospective sellers.

Awarding the contract to the lowest bidder may be asking for trouble later on as the lowest bidder may not have good understanding of the work.

Cancelling a bid and re-advertising is a lengthy and expensive process. Without knowing what caused current variations, you may end up with the same situation again.

Who is the best supplier? The one who has the best understanding of the work and has the capability to deliver it. Price difference is big and it will be almost impossible to determine who the best bidder is.

67: A

A developer's absence of 5 days due to illness will impact schedule directly so this is a schedule constraint. Unclear specifications resulted in low quality work directly so this is a quality constraint. Tester's per day cost being higher impacts the budget directly so this is a budget constraint. A programmer being less experienced than expected impacts productivity which is directly related to resource and may have indirect impact on schedule/budget/quality. Therefore, this is the BEST choice of being a resource constraint.

68: C

Best action is to recommend a change to the company's training policy to allow training for temporary project resources. This will not just help the current project but future projects too. Waiving training is same as having untrained resources and the result of that is already evident from high number of defects. So that is an incorrect approach. If internal trained programmers were available for project work that would have been the first choice. The reason to hire temporary programmers was that internal resources were not available. Training temporary resources on coding standards is against the company policy whether the formal training is conducted or a brief presentation is provided.

69: C

There is no need to take any action as the resource outage happened when the resource was not needed but is expected to be back to work when the resource has to start project work. Calling resource to let him know that he needs to return on time is not a prudent choice. It shows lack of confidence in the resource or as if he is away on purpose. No need for a replacement resource as no work is being affected. Also there is no need to add contingency to the schedule.

70: C

Functional organization provides almost no authority. Same is the case with weak matrix where project manager may have somewhat authority over resources from own department but minimal over resources from other departments. Strong matrix organization gives considerably much more authority to project manager compared to balanced matrix organization, as project manager has a direct hierarchy to the management separate from other departments and this provides them the support needed.

71: D

Government regulations require public invitation to sellers for certain types of contracts. This seems to be the best reason why project manager advertised. The question is asking why advertise when you have six reputed sellers known to you. So whether it is newspaper or internet, the cost of advertising is not the issue. Using advertising to delay the award of the contract is an unethical choice. Best seller would be someone who meets the criteria and from the question it seems all six meet the criteria.

72: C

Each project is unique and so are stakeholder's expectations and needs. So the plan should be used as a template and modified to fit the current project. Project quality management plan is the responsibility of the project manager and not the customer. Creating a new plan from scratch will result in a lot of unnecessary effort which can be saved by using old plan as a template.

73: A

Once bid solicitation process is completed, the contract is awarded to the selected contractor. Advertisement is a tool used in bid solicitation process. Creation of qualified sellers' list happens before bid solicitation starts. Prospective sellers' proposals are received during bid solicitation process.

74: A

Validate Scope process does not ensure project completes on time and within budget. It also does not differentiate between change request work and other deliverables. Though it is concerned with meeting business requirements, it is definitely not involved with realizing business benefits.

75: B

The five stages in the above case, in order, are: forming, storming, norming, performing, and adjourning. The other three choices are incorrect as storming happens before norming and there is no such stage as adjusting.

76: B

In planning process group, project management plan is developed and not carried out as such. In monitoring and controlling process group, work performance is compared against project management plan. Resource leveling has to do with schedule modifications considering resource constraints. In executing process group, project management plans are carried out by coordinating resources.

77: A

Whenever a contract is completed or terminated for any reason, the Close Procurements process has to be started to close the contract. Controlling Procurements process is finished when the decision to terminate the contract has been made and the Close Procurements process starts. There is no need for negotiations as the decision to terminate has already been made. Dispute may or may not result from contract termination so it cannot be said that disputes will be triggered.

78: A

After risk analysis has been done, a risk response strategy has to be established for all the risks that require a response according to the plan. Developing risk response strategy for the technology projects only is not the right approach since non-technology risk can materialize and become an issue.

79: B

Group creativity techniques include Mind mapping and Affinity diagram methods since both require a group working. Group decision making techniques are dictatorship, unanimity, majority, and plurality. Stakeholder analysis techniques include salience model, power/influence grid, etc. Observation technique can also be called as job shadowing.

80: D

Constraints are limitations or boundaries and not necessarily difficulties. Assumptions are assumed facts that may or may not be real but are considered to be real. Risks are potential difficulties that may or may not be faced by the project and may not necessarily hinder the team's ability to meet project goals. Issues are the difficulties that are being faced and that can hinder the project team's ability to achieve project goals.

81: A

Implementing the approved changes is done in the Direct and Manage Project Work process. All the other three are done in Perform Integrated Change Control process.

82: D

Risk mitigation planning comes after risks have been analyzed. Customer's experience is of value but cannot be the tool that can be used in isolation. Risk register is for recording risks not analyzing them. Expert judgment includes customer's experience and project team's experience so this is the best choice.

83: B

Plans are prepared for the purpose of executing them so project management plan is executed in the Direct and Manage Project Work process. All the other three belong to monitoring and controlling process group.

84: C

Only in the projectized organization the project team members will be worried about their next assignment during the project close phase since they report directly to project manager in the hierarchy of the organization and their sole assignment is to work on projects. If there are no more projects, their services will no longer be required.

85: C

Approve project charter is not a process. Collect requirements is part of planning process. Initiation is what initiating process group does. Develop Project Charter and Identify Stakeholders are the two processes of Initiating process group.

86: B

A deliverable is a unique and verifiable product, result, or capability. An activity is the task needed to be performed as part of creating the deliverable. An objective is what is achieved or is expected to be achieved through a deliverable. An action item is same thing as an activity but exists outside the project activities list. Usually it is a sub-activity to complete an activity.

87: B

Program Evaluation and Review Technique (PERT) is an estimation technique that is not directly used for forecasting project budget at completion. The other three techniques are directly used for this purpose.

88: C

Acquisition, multi criteria decision analysis, and negotiation are the tools and techniques of Acquire Project Team process. Networking is not one of the tools or techniques though may indirectly have an impact when using the Acquire Project Team process tools and techniques.

89: A

There is no scope verification document in itself. The information is available in scope management plan. Statement of work contains the work to be completed not how it will be verified. Communications management plan describes how and when communications will occur.

90: C

Bidders' conference happens in Conduct Procurements process. Statement of work is created and contract terms are defined in the Plan Procurement Management process. Managing the contractual relationship between buyer and seller is what happens in Control Procurements process.

91: D

This happens in the Norming stage where the team has better understanding of the work to be performed and good idea of how the project is to be managed. So in this stage, the team members start to understand others' work styles and adjust their work habits for smooth interactions within the team. In Performing stage, team works as a well-oiled machine. There is no stage that is called adjusting.

92: D

As assumption is something that is believed to be true though it may not be true. Among the four options, there are three assumptions viz. entire team fluent in English language, all resources are technically competent, and costs in all countries is within budget. Only entire team's fluency in English is an assumption related to communications planning. The others are related to resources and cost planning. Team members acquired in various geographical locations is not an assumption but a fact.

93: D

The best thing to do is to build the team with a fresh start by defining clear roles and responsibilities so that every team member understands his/her and others responsibilities. Also create a reward system to motivate team members to perform well.

Letting few members go and bringing in new members will be more detrimental to the team morale which is already very low.

Team development is not a core project management process so it will be very difficult to convince management to extend the schedule or budget for this activity; besides the focus should be on taking positive steps to improve morale. Bringing into management notice may not be a motivator for the team.

The scenario does not mention any issue with WBS so there is no need to recreate WBS. This will be a waste of time and may actually result in lowering team morale further.

94: C

3 resources working for 6 hours/day = 18 hours planned value of work per day

18 x 8 days = 144 hours planned value of work until the end of 8th day

The 'twelve days' information is extra and not needed to find the solution.

95: B

The biggest benefit of colocation that is lost is the concept of a team. Instant messaging and daily conference calls may help with reporting but will have minimal impact on the lost benefit of colocation. Coming in once a week can definitely help with team building but may be difficult to manage as all team members have to come to office on the same day. This may also involve expense on a continuing basis which could be a constraint. The most productive step will be to bring the team members together and develop the notion of a team among them. Bringing them together for an offsite event will help them socialize with each other and develop a relationship. This is, therefore, the best choice.

96: B

Risks are what may happen not what will happen. If you are certain something will happen then it is not a risk but a constraint. It may not have happened in the previous projects but can happen in this project. It is obvious that Identify Risks process identifies risks to the project. But this is a weak answer.

97: D

Once the final deliverable has been accepted by the customer, the work has been completed. This happens in Validate Scope process. Monitoring and Controlling process group is where the Validate Scope process happens. Therefore, at completion the Closing Project process is to be started to formally close the project. Control Communications mostly happens on a regular basis and is independent of acceptance of final deliverable or process.

98: B

Executing process group is where the actual work is performed to complete the deliverables of the project. No matter what the project type is, whether expensive equipment is deployed or high cost material is used or only resources work on the project, the main expense happens in executing process group.

99: D

You have transferred the risk to the insurance company. Of course there is a cost associated with that which is the cost of insurance, but that cost will be much less than the cost incurred due to delay of work.

100: C

No matter what the project is, the project or project phase is authorized to proceed in Develop Project Charter process. Though Develop Project Charter process is part of initiating process group, it is a better choice since it is more specific than initiating process group. The other two choices are wrong.

101: A

Each person has different communication needs so the most effective step the project manager can take in this scenario is to understand the communication needs of the new sponsor and update the communication plan to reflect that. With a new role, understanding project details in a meeting or self-accessing project repository will be the last thing on new sponsor's mind. Both will prove to be pretty much ineffective. Sending project status report without understanding what type and how frequent communication the sponsor is expecting, will be ineffective.

102: D

She is comparing how much contingency reserve is left and what is the amount of the remaining risks on the project. Just finding out how much has been spent and how much reserve is remaining does not provide any value. Comparison of spend on managing risks versus other spends or contingency reserve spend versus management reserve spend is not part of reserve analysis and does not provide much value.

103: B

Risks are not certain though these are believed to represent reality. Deadlines and constraints are certain and not just considered certain. Only assumptions are considered to be certain though in reality they may not be Hence assumptions is the correct choice.

104: B

A regulation and court order are directives usually for repeated use but these do not focus on organization or increasing probability of success. A best practice increases probability of success and reduces chances of error but does not necessarily focus on organization. A standard, on the other hand, provides guidelines for common and repeated use. The purpose is to be more organized so as to reduce errors and increase chances of success. Standard provides minimum acceptable value of results.

105: B

The role of CCB should be clearly defined within the configuration control and change control procedures. This helps in going through the process smoothly without any lost time. CCB is not part of project manager's role and responsibilities so should not be included there. There is no need to have detailed contact information of all CCB members. Usually CCB meetings and reviews are initiated by an assigned member who receives the change request for review and approval. Having CCB on the intranet does not really make sense. Depending on organization's information system, CCB meetings could be held online/virtual/face-to-face.

106: C

Re-kickoff meeting will not be helpful in better coordination until some organization is done. Even if the acceptance criteria of deliverables exist, without any organization not much can be accomplished. Lessons learned exercise is of more value for future projects but can also provide benefits to the current project. Selecting a project life cycle and defining clear roles and responsibilities will put the project on the path to success and, as such, is the most important step needed in this situation. After this, a re-kickoff can be arranged, a lessons learned exercise can be done, and acceptance criteria of each deliverable can be developed.

107: C

Team development needs to happen in any environment or organizational structure. Even a team working together in operational role needs to be developed because new challenges and issues arise all the time, which require that some effort is spent on further developing or re-developing the team. When the whole team reports to one functional manager, it becomes much easier and simpler to manage the team development as the functional manager is well aware of the needs and strengths of each team member. Comparatively, in a projectized organization, though the whole team reports to one project manager, the team itself is together only for the project and sometimes a few projects. This makes team development more challenging.

108: C

'Managing risks' means managing uncertainty. Unknown risks cannot be managed because those are not known so there is nothing to manage. Though risk management is part of project management but that cannot be the reason for using it. To identify and analyze risks and then develop responses is what is done when doing risk management, not the reason why it is being done.

109: B

If a completed deliverable is rejected by the sponsor/customer, a change request may be required to fix the defects so that it can be resubmitted for acceptance. Validation of change request completion is part of the integrated change control process. Change requests do not result from acceptance of deliverables but rejection of deliverables.

110: D

Procurement audit is done when the contract work has been completed so it is performed during Close Procurements process. It does not make sense to do procurement audit in Close Project or Phase. Those are independent of each other. Conduct Procurements is when sellers are selected and contract is awarded. Control Procurements is when contract is being performed. Both processes occur too early to perform an audit of the procurement.

111: B

Requirements for Close Procurements process will be found in the project documents. So enterprise environmental factors have nothing to do with it. The statement of work is what work is to be delivered so that is also not a choice. Procurement change control system provides the process of how contract changes will be managed. Terms of the contract provide the conditions and steps involved for various processes including the Close Procurements process. This is the correct choice.

112: D

Activity	Duration	Predecessor	Cost of Activity	Cost of Crashing (per day)	Max Days it can be Crashed
A	7		2,000	200	0
B	9	A	3,000	200	2
C	8	B	2,000	300	2
D	9	C	4,000	300	3
E	5	C	3,000	500	3
F	4	D,E	1,000	100	0

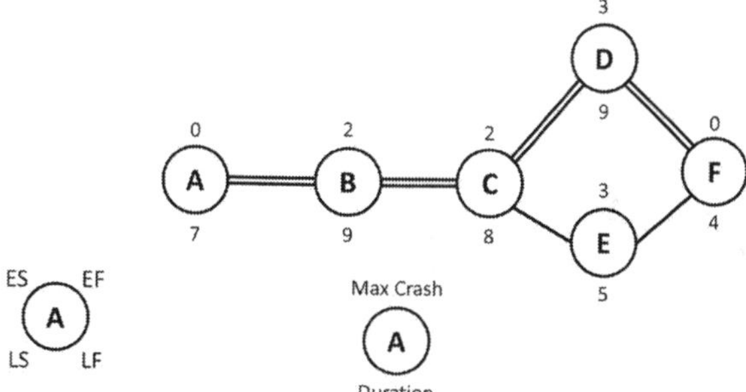

Critical Path is 37 days. So crashing the schedule by seven days can be achieved by crashing activities B, C, D (2+2+3) for a cost of (2 x 200 + 2 x 300 + 3 x 300) = $1,900.

113: A

Crashing non-critical tasks will not help in schedule compression so the focus should be to crash critical tasks only. Crashing the tasks that have the highest costs has no impact on schedule compression especially if the tasks are not on critical path. Besides cost is not an issue so this cannot be the best choice.

114: A

Management by walking around (MBWA) is not directly about quality but mainly about motivating employees. Hence the project quality management area does not include MBWA concepts.

115: A

It does not disallow scope changes just regulates those. Ambiguous scope is not the only reason why scope creep occurs. The other three choices are correct about the Control Scope process.

116: A

Plan Procurement Management is an input to identify stakeholder process because the contract identifies the key stakeholders. Collect Requirements happen after stakeholder identification since the identified stakeholders are contacted to collect requirements. Change log and Plan Quality Management have no role to play in stakeholder identification.

117: B

Strategic plan does not list individual projects rather overall goals of the organization and the high level approach of how these goals will be achieved. Project charter provides high level list of a project's milestones and/or activities. Portfolio charter is more about the approach portfolio management is taking and usually does not list the projects to be executed. Program charter will include list of all related projects that are being managed together. Therefore this is the right choice.

118: B

Explicitly means that constraints and assumptions are clearly defined and implicitly means not directly mentioned but understood well. So defining activities would be considered implicitly.

119: D

The best use of Estimate At Completion (EAC) and Estimate To Complete (ETC) is for forecasting. These can be derived from schedule performance data and/or cost performance data. These do have some value in the lessons learned but their most beneficial use is as a forecast.

120: A

Proposal evaluation criteria are established in Plan Procurement Management process. Contract negotiation happens in Conduct Procurements process. Litigation is not the main tool used in the Control Procurements process as it happens in very few cases. The main tool is the contract change control system which is established for each and every procurement and is often used.

121: A

Develop schedule process will be least impacted by scope and cost of the project. This is because their impact has already been taken care of by the estimating process. Constraints have to be considered explicitly so that everyone is clear of the limitations. Lead time and lag time do not impact schedule development as these are incorporated into the schedule. Forced milestones and external deadlines will put constraints on the schedule and the schedule must be able to accommodate those in most cases.

122: A

Evaluation criteria is established in the Plan Procurement Management process but she is going through the Conduct Procurements process at this time so this is incorrect. Control Procurements process starts once the contract has been awarded. There is no process called Initiate Procurements.

123: B

In strong matrix organization, project manager has more authority than in any other type of organization except the projectized organization. The other three statements are all correct.

124: A

To build a new system is definitely project work so it cannot be considered operational work. Several projects can be directed at different aspects of the information system, but pretty much have well defined deliverables attached to these. Since the overall building of the system has a very specific outcome already defined, this is a large project with various sub-projects and should not be considered as a program.

125: B

Inflating task estimates is a bad practice as it hides the actual estimate and thus weakens the control. Threatening that you will not manage the project will likely result in your removal from the project and maybe even from the company. The purpose of contingency reserve is to provide funds for known risks. A high reserve will raise eyebrows and unnecessary questions and must be justified. With a 25% of budget added to contingency, it will be extremely difficult to justify. Actual cost estimate should be presented with a brief that provides explanation of what will be the impact on the project if the budget is cut.

126: C

Project performance baselines are developed in the planning process group while project charter is developed in the initiating process group which happens before planning starts. The other three choices are used to develop the project charter.

127: A

Expert judgment is not a tool and technique of the Manage Stakeholder Engagement process.

128: A

SPI greater than 1.0 means the project is ahead of schedule.

129: A

Analyzing activity durations to produce the project schedule is done in Develop Schedule process so this is not an objective of Control Schedule process.

130: D

Roles and responsibilities, terms and conditions, and list of deliverables are all required as part of the contract since these define what is to be delivered, how and by whom. Work breakdown structure is not required and would be least valuable as part of the contract.

131: D

It is to develop good working relationship with the seller. Pressurize the seller to do more work for the same money or push to reduce the price can backfire later even though the seller may agree at the time. This is not a good practice. Terms and conditions were already reviewed and were part of the sellers' proposal. Changing terms at this time can only be to bring clarity and can be done. But this is not the best choice.

132: A

The company should select the new product development project because it has the highest internal rate of return of 25 percent.

133: B

The change does not really add value so you should refuse to upsell something knowing that it is of no value. No need to evaluate budget and schedule impact as you do not recommend this change. This is not scope creep. The scenario actually mentions extending scope, budget and time which means it will be processed as a change request if agreed to.

134: C

Pareto chart is a type of histogram where defects, for example, are sorted by type from highest occurring to lowest ones. PERT is an estimation technique and not a chart. Control chart is drawn against time, not by frequency of occurrence. Bar Chart is also drawn against time and is not a histogram. Over a period of time these show activities and not the defects.

135: B

Risk register updates and corrective action in the form of change request are the output of the process. Contingent response strategies, if being referred to contingency planning, is an output of Plan Risk Response process. Meetings is the tool used in Control Risks process.

136: A

Activity	Planned Value (PV)	Actual Cost (AC)	Earned Value (EV)	CPI	SPI
A	1,200	1,000	1,100	1.1	0.9
B	600	500	600	1.2	1.0
C	300	300	300	1.0	1.0
D	1,800	2,000	1,800	0.9	1.0

Cost Performance Index (CPI) = Earned Value (EV) / Actual Cost (AC) and

Schedule Performance Index (SPI) = Earned Value (EV) / Planned Value (PV)

Activity B and C, both are on time and within budget but activity B is doing better on budget compared to activity C. So Activity B is the right answer.

137: C

Once the contract is terminated, the first thing to do is start the Close Procurements process. This is the responsibility of the project manager so this action has to be taken. Control Procurements process already got completed when the contract got terminated. Restarting Conduct Procurement process is wrong even if the management decided to hire a new seller.

138: C

Instant messaging in not needed for co-located team members. Distributing contact information to the whole team is not too helpful when the team is co-located. Sending the technical team lead for training can be done only if this is a major weakness for that individual but is irrelevant to the team being co-located or not. Having all team members participate in creating a work breakdown structure is an excellent way to develop the team and bring the team members together.

139: C

Engaging a seller though a contract is a time consuming and expensive process so cancelling contract for a missed deliverable is not prudent without giving a notification and a chance to the seller to correct the issue. Similarly issuing a warning before any communication on missed deliverable seems too aggressive and can damage the relationship. The creation of interview schedule is the responsibility of the seller and as such should be created by seller to avoid unnecessary complications. The best choice is to ask the seller to stop the work and submit the schedule for approval. Once the schedule is approved, the work can be restarted based on the schedule.

140: A

Installing an electric outlet is part of the scope so adding another outlet is adding additional work to the scope of the project. Since no information has been given whether integrated change control process is being followed or not, this will be adding unauthorized scope and hence will result in scope creep. There is no mention of cost or schedule so both cost overrun and schedule delay are incorrect choices. Micro-management is a relative term and since there is no mention of what and how the project was to be managed, it cannot be considered micro-managed when a scope addition is requested.

141: D

Aggressive schedule and tight budget means the risks are much higher. So he is seeking risks or taking on more risks.

142: B

Establish cost baseline by including estimates is not an objective of controlling cost of project. Cost baseline is established by the Determine Budget process.

143: B

It is the Administrative Closure procedure in the Close Project or Phase process. Quality assurance is an executing process and it checks sufficiency of quality plan and measurements. Validate scope is a monitoring and controlling process that is concerned with acceptance of deliverables and gets confirmation from the sponsor that exit criteria has been satisfied. It does not talk about project or phase acceptance. Stakeholders' define their need with the help of the project team but project team mainly defines, working with stakeholders, how these needs will be met. This choice does not refer to any process and is more of a general statement.

144: C

Duration of a project, project environment, and urgency of the need of information, all can impact the type and frequency of use of communication technology. For example, a short duration project vs. a long duration project may require use of instant messaging and phone more frequently. Similarly, a co-located vs. remote team will impact the type of communication technology in use. A seller's proposal does not have any impact since it has to be a formal written communication. So this is the right choice.

145: B

A change request that fixes the problem by bringing future performance in line with the project management plan is a corrective action. An action that reduces the probability of negative consequences of risks is a preventive action. An approved change request was submitted before it was processed and approved but no longer can be called as submitted change request. There is no change request defined as supportive action.

146: D

Next step is to implement the approved change. Change request is only closed once the approved change has been implemented and validated. Recommending corrective action is part of the integrated change control process. Question is what happens afterwards? Preventive actions may or may not be published but this is something that does not make the project move forward. Implementing the change request does help the project.

147: B

The appropriate action is to review the quality plan, the filled checklists and the problems identified by design team, to see where the root of the problem is. This is essentially quality assurance which checks the adequacy of the quality management processes. Reproducing the documents for 4 departments may fix those documents but does not guarantee that the rest will not have issues. Sharing the checklist with design team or rejecting the design team's objection does not improve the quality of the documents.

148: B

The creation of statement of work, which is identifying deliverables which can be achieved through sellers, happens in the Plan Procurement Management process so the project manager must be in Plan Procurement Management process. Control Procurements process follows Conduct Procurements process which follows the Plan Procurement Management process.

149: A

Absolutely. Completed deliverables must be validated at end of each phase before project moves to next phase. You do not need sponsor's approval since this is an essential part of deliverable completion. Even though customer may or may not have been reviewing deliverables as these were being completed, these still need to be formally accepted by the sponsor/customer. Deliverables, due in a phase, mostly are handed over and accepted by the customer at the end of that phase. In this case if the customer is asking for that, then there is no reason to delay till the end of the project. Actually it will increase the risk if delayed till project end.

150: A

This is an example of expert power where a project manager asks for your advice because he believes that you have the knowledge and experience to guide him well. There is no indication of formal or coercive power display in this scenario. There is no such thing as management power.

151: A

Legal settlement is the agreement by both parties on certain dispute. 'Control Procurements' happens before formal written notice of completion is given. Close project or phase is too generalized as it deals with the whole project not necessarily with completion of a contract. Close Procurements is the process where the seller is provided with formal written notice of completion of a legal agreement.

152: A

Project planning may take too long when focus is lost. This can happen if the project manager has weak management skills. There is less chance of developing an aggressive schedule when project team members are directly involved. Team will generally resist building an aggressive schedule. A realistic achievable plan can also be developed by the project manager with minimal involvement from project team members. However, this can be considered an outcome of involving project team members. When project team members are involved in project planning, they will know what they are to do, when, and how; this will save significant amount of project manager's time. This is because project manager spends most time in coordinating and communicating. This is a better and certain choice compared to the other ones.

153: B

Keeping lessons learned review confidential is detrimental to the project. The document should be distributed to all project stakeholders for their information and feedback. This way the document benefits the stakeholders by improving their understanding of the project and helps current project from their input. It also incorporates their input to make this document a more effective one for future projects.

Publishing lessons learned in companywide newsletter will not be valuable as only project stakeholders are interested in the project information and they are the ones that can contribute to the document.

Individual performance review is not a lessons learned objective. Actually it should never be used for that as team members will be reserved in making suggestions and bringing the issues to light.

154: A

The formula to determine channels of communications is:
Number of channels = n(n-1)/2 where n is the number of stakeholders
So, originally there were 6 team members which means,
6(6-1)/2 = 15 channels
Now there are 11 team members, so
11(11-1)/2 = 55 channels.
Therefore, an additional (55-11) = 40 channels have been added.

155: C

The purpose of a template is to help the project save time and money and/or reduce the chances of error. Therefore, template cannot be considered a project constraint.

156: A

Multiple sponsors managing the project is the main area of concern. If this continues it can make decision making and sponsor intervention much more difficult. Reports can be sent to all four so that is not an issue. There is no mention of a matrix environment, so this cannot be the best choice. Identifying who will accept the deliverables is part of identifying one sponsor for the project.

157: A

Work authorization system is used to ensure tasks are performed at the right time and in the proper sequence. So either this system is not established or is not working properly. WBS, communication plan, and team coordination do not have a role in ensuring work done at the right time and in correct sequence.

158: C

There is no need to update business case and project charter. The change to those two documents is only needed if there is a significant change to the project objectives. Approved changes cannot be tracked against the cost and schedule baselines if the baselines have not been updated to reflect the changes. Work authorization system sequences and authorizes work. The work has to be included in the project plan before it can be performed. Therefore, updating cost and schedule baselines to reflect the changes is the first thing that should be done.

159: B

Project management processes do not specify or create project's product. This is done by product oriented processes. Project management processes may or may not be more complex than product oriented processes. Both interact and overlap throughout the project lifecycle. Both project management and product oriented processes have a definite start and an end. The objective of project management processes compared to product oriented processes is that these ensure project flows smoothly through to completion.

160: B

The question asks increasing the acceptance of deliverables not speeding the acceptance of deliverables. Therefore, offering discount on fees for quick deliverable acceptance is a wrong choice.

The deliverables are accepted when they appear to meet the requirements. The more clearly it shows that they meet the acceptance criteria the more chances that the deliverables will be accepted. So sending a written request to accept deliverables does not impact appearance of meeting acceptance criteria.

Stakeholders cannot define deliverables without intervention and help by the project team since project team is the one that has to agree and complete the deliverables. This is a weak choice.

Involving stakeholders during initiation increases the understanding of both the project deliverables and their acceptance criteria; this includes all stakeholders including the project team. This has a direct impact on acceptance of deliverables as stakeholders have a clearer understanding of what is being delivered and how it meets the criteria.

161: C

Only project resources that are being charged to the project should be fully included in the budget. Some resources working on the project may not get charged against the project. The expense may be coming out of an operational budget while the resource is partially working on the project. Same is the case of equipment. The equipment used on the project may be expensed from an operational budget. Payments made to the vendor for the contract work done for the project, and included in the statement of work to be paid from project budget, will be part of the budget. But the statement "All payments made to the vendor" is vague and can include any expense. For example, annual license fee paid to the vendor may come out of operational budget rather than project budget.

162: D

Control Risks process is where risks are monitored whether these are residual or not. This process also ensures continuous risk identification throughout the project life cycle. Identify risks and plan risk management does not include monitoring residual risks. So these two options are incorrect. There is no process called as residual risk management.

163: A

Active listening, collaboration, and negotiation are all extremely important skills for an effective project manager. Body language though is a good and needed skill but may not be that important compared to the other three because project manager's communication happens through face-to-face, phone, email, and written reports. Please note that the question is asking for the LEAST important skill among the four.

164: C

All four are examples of project records. With regards to communications, project records include all documents that describe and explain the project and any method of physical or electronic organization of such documents/information. Electronic databases and filing systems are used for organizing information not communicating it. None of these is a project deliverable unless the project is about creating a web based project dashboard, a filing system, or an electronic database.

165: C

Pareto chart is a tool and technique not an input to the process.

166: D

Cost Variance (CV) = Earned Value (EV) - Actual Cost (AC)
Since both EV and AC are known, CV can be calculated as follows:
CV = 24,000 - 19,500 = +4,500

167: C

You are upset because scope control process was not followed. Though the decision may seem good it may have repercussions later on because neither complete review and analysis was performed nor its impact on all other project deliverables was considered. Reduced profit and exclusion from decision making are wrong reasons to be upset. Deliverables can be changed once baselined but through following the integrated change control process, not on the fly.

168: B

Decision tree analysis is used to analyze various options and not to make a group decision. This could be used as a tool to help with decision making but in itself is not a decision making technique.

169: A

The documentation of the acceptance also occurs in the same process. i.e. Validate Scope process. Close Project or Phase occurs after completion of deliverable acceptance including completion of documentation. Control Procurements is for deliverables completed by seller under a contract only. So this cannot be the complete answer. Perform quality assurance is unrelated to deliverable acceptance.

170: A

When estimating is done at activity level and then summed up for the project, it is called bottom-up estimating. When estimating is done at higher level and distributed down to activities, it is called top-down estimating. Though expert judgment is used in parametric estimating, it alone cannot make a good estimate. Taking into account considerable historical data provides a good basis to perform parametric estimating.

171: C

Finish-to-Start is the most common activity to activity relationship used. In fact, some schedules if not needed to be fast tracked are built entirely with this relationship.

172: A

A control chart is the best tool for this purpose as it shows the measurements and deviation from acceptable limits. Fishbone diagram and Pareto Chart are used to identify the root cause of an issue and major issues respectively. Scatter diagram shows relationship between two factors and does not show against a standard.

173: A

Influence/Impact grid is used for classifying the stakeholders after they have been identified. This happens in Identify Stakeholders process.

174: C

Run chart and statistical sampling are quality control tools and techniques. Benchmarking is a quality planning technique. Therefore, expert judgment is the best choice which can identify how and when quality assurance activity should be performed in order to have minimum project disruptions and maximum benefits realization.

175: C

A project team should never deliver more than what stakeholders are expecting because of two main reasons. One, the value of extra functionality or additional delivery is very little in the eyes of the stakeholders because they believe they do not need it. Second, trying to deliver extra can backfire by putting the in-scope work at risk of being late, over budget or prone to defects.

176: A

Defining activities has WBS as an input but sequencing activities does not need WBS. Both Plan Quality Management and Estimate Costs benefit from WBS as an input.

177: B

Scope addition means a change request has to be processed and approved; therefore such communication should be formal written. Instant messaging is an informal written communication so cannot be considered for the purpose of a change request. Formal or informal verbal communication and informal written communication are inappropriate in this situation.

178: D

Make or buy decision is needed to plan the project approach so it is a part of the planning process. Hence it cannot be an input to planning or initiating process groups. Monitoring and controlling has to do with comparing performance against baseline. Once a make or buy decision is made, the project usually does not track whether the decision was right or not. Besides such decision's impact usually lasts beyond the project. Therefore this seems to be a weak choice. The decision of make or buy is implemented in executing process group so it is definitely an input to the executing process group. This is the best choice.

179: D

General management skills include being an effective negotiator, motivator, leader, and a good listener but it does not really address the skills of being highly flexible and be able to compromise to achieve project objectives. A project manager without this skill is very likely to fail.

180: B

The deliverables are accepted through Validate Scope process. Once all the deliverables have been accepted, these become input to the Close Project or Phase process. Administrative closure is part of the Close Project or Phase process. Integrated change control is for managing submitted change requests and not for accepting deliverables. There is no such process as accept scope.

181: D

The project team prepares the bid package and advertisement and then spends the effort on advertising. Arbitrator does not even exist at this stage.

Sponsor has minimal involvement. Prospective sellers get involved once the bids are advertised.

182: A

In cause effect diagram, problems or potential problems are linked to the factors. The effects are linked to the causes. So this is the best choice. In process analysis, non-value added work is identified. Through Pareto chart, highest occurring problems are identified. Quality assurance checks compliance against company's quality policies.

183: C

Sellers who have failed to deliver in the past may not be responsible for the failure. Hence simply disqualifying a seller based on that may result in losing a well suited seller. Fixed price contracts are less risky when the requirements are well defined and articulated, otherwise shifting the risk to the seller does not mean project will be successful. Procurement planning starts along with general project management planning as it is part of that. Going through make-or-buy decision is a good practice because it helps analyze what are the risks involved in doing the work in-house versus asking seller to deliver the work. So this is the correct choice.

184: B

The resource availability information goes into resource calendar not activity attributes. This is the right choice. Schedule baseline will be modified only if the absence is affecting the project. Same is the case with critical path; No change unless the baselines are affected. Resource non-availability may change the critical path. This is a weak choice since it has so many conditions to it. Without having any prior commitment or knowing the impact, it will be unwise to simply refuse the resource from going on vacation.

185: B

Work performance data and earned value measurements are only available once the execution processes start. Since the question is asking about planning phase, the three choices with these two items are incorrect. Hence, the correct choice is report format and level of detail.

186: A

She has already identified that project lacked proper communication. So she should create a communication plan that defines what information needs to be distributed and obtained and when this should happen. Then start implementing this communication plan.

Performing a quality audit will be an overkill since she already knows that it is a communication problem. Fix that first and then if there still are problems, audit can be used as a tool to uncover that.

Informing stakeholders' of what has been missing without a plan as to how this will be fixed is a bad idea and will just reduce stakeholder satisfaction and confidence in project manager.

First, issue log is updated by the project team not all stakeholders. So sending an email to stakeholders does not make much sense in this regard. Beside this step will not produce any results to fix the issue at hand.

187: D

Crashing and Fast tracking are the two ways a schedule can be compressed. Resource leveling actually extends the schedule rather than compressing it. Schedule networking is irrelevant here.

188: D

There may not be enough information available for quality work in the new phase when project phases overlap. Such work may include planning and execution that need to be redone once more information becomes available. Sequential relationship will provide complete information moving from one phase to another. There is no such type of phase called as integrated Iterative is a type of life cycle where project phases are repeated. It can be sequential or overlapping.

189: B

For a new project, identification of stakeholders happens in the Initiating process group. Though it continues throughout the project life cycle, Initiating process group is the best choice.

190: A

Lessons learned are the historical records of past projects to help improve future project performance. All the other three have the main objective of improving current project's performance.

191: D

The first thing you should do is evaluate the impact of resource capability on project cost and schedule. After that, you can either request for more resources or submit a change request since you now know what needs to be done to achieve project goals. You can also speak with the buyer to alleviate his concerns because you now know what the impact is and how you will manage it.

192: A

Project charter is the output of Develop Project Charter process. Deliverables, work performance data, and change requests are all outputs of Direct and Manage Project Work process.

193: A

It is project manager's responsibility to ensure that products or services acquired from the seller under a contract meet the needs of the project and also comply with business policies of the buyer. Legal counsel ensures that the contract is sound, valid and executable. Project sponsor is minimally involved with procurements. The seller is only responsible for delivering the products or services under the contract and cannot be held responsible whether these meet the business policies of the buyer.

194: B

Project scope and product scope are not the same concepts so product scope is not a subset of project scope. Project scope, not product scope, is the work needed to deliver the product on time, within budget and within scope. Product scope is a combination of product scopes of smaller components since each component in itself is a product.

195: A

Team building, communications, and conflict resolution are more challenging when team members are not collocated. Reporting would be the least challenging among the four choices, because it follows a set process and involves comparatively less soft skills than the other three choices.

196: B

Project manager manages the project so he/she cannot be the one who authorizes it. Project management office, sponsor, or portfolio manager can authorize the project depending on the process established for this purpose in an organization.

197: B

Control risks process is concerned with managing risks and hence does not use earned value management technique. Direct and Manage Project Work process only measures and provides work performance data but does not use earned value technique. Manage Communications process occurs after the earned value technique has been used to understand performance variances. Control costs process is the right choice since it uses the earned value management technique to understand performance variances.

198: C

Project quality assurance report identifies where the project plan does not follow company policies and procedures. Executive report is a very general term but may refer to project status report prepared for executive audience. The project performance report provides the status of the project progress. Quality control report will show measurements compared against project standards.

199: C

Developing cost performance baseline is done in the Determine Budget process of the Planning process group. Controlling communications can be called as an objective of developing cost performance baseline but not the other way around.

200: B

Standard Deviation (SD) = (Pessimistic - Optimistic) /6
SD = (24 - 12) / 6 = 2

6 - ANSWERS & EXPLANATIONS TEST 2

1: D

Halo effect is a cognitive bias that results in generalizing a person's performance in one area and applying it to another area. So a programmer getting promoted to project manager because of successful performance in programming area is a good example of that.

2: C

Thanking manager in the email which is about project team's performance seems flattering and out of context.

Fixing project problems especially when it is impacting the whole organization does not require permission of the manager. It is the responsibility of the project manager.

Emergency issues, like the one mentioned, do not need to go through integrated change control process. The purpose of integrated change control process is not to force the following of the process but to realize better business benefits.

The manager is disappointed that even after ensuring and taking preventive measures, such a widespread issue has occurred. His concern is why and how did the team fail in realizing this potential problem even when they have put significant effort into it.

3: A

The purpose of using earned value management is to measure performance. It provides us with variances from plans and schedule. Performance indices provide us the basis to forecast future performance.

4: C

The seller is charging for the time a resource spends on the contract/project, therefore this must be a time and material contract. In cost reimbursable and cost plus fixed fee contracts, the actual cost of the resources will be reimbursed not a negotiated price.

5: C

Both coding the software program and testing are part of the actual work being done by following the project management plan. So it happens in Executing process group.

6: C

It does not make sense to restart the whole project. The work that has already completed would be a waste in this case: loss of time and money. All others are valid options.

7: A

Market trend is an external factor that is impacting the objectives of the project. The change has occurred due to external factors. Scope definition, requirements, and project budget are not the factors impacting this change.

8: A

Since the change evaluation and project decisions are being made by a functional manager, your role is that of an expediter even though your title may be project manager.

In general, in the presence of a project manager, if the management starts to interfere with project decision making, it will be difficult for the project manager to keep the project in control. Team morale can also get impacted and several other problems can raise their head.

Manager's concern to satisfy stakeholders should be directed to project manager. The communication needs of the manager may include something like how stakeholders' needs are being satisfied.

This is definitely not integrated change control. The change was approved through an informal discussion between the manager and the key user. No impact analysis was done and no documentation was created.

9: D

Executing process is all about managing resources, human or otherwise. So this is where the focus should be. Performing the project work is not the focus of the project manager generally unless he/she is responsible for that too in a small project team. Even then, as project manager, the focus should be on managing resources. Measuring progress is a secondary activity. Conflict resolution is a controlling activity.

10: C

Budget At Completion (BAC) = $1,000,000

Actual Cost (AC) = $650,000

Without knowing Cost Performance Index, Cost Variance, earned value cannot be known. It can be $650,000 if CPI = 1.0

It cannot be the cost variance since CV = EV - AC

Though it is a design build project, there is no mention of this expense being a design cost. So this choice is incorrect.

$650,000 has been spent and cannot be recovered. This money is called the sunk cost.

11: D

Scope statement is created in the planning process which occurs after project charter has been approved; therefore SOW cannot be part of the scope statement.

12: C

Plan Procurement Management is the process where procurement management plan is developed and bid package is prepared. After that in Conduct Procurements process, sellers' responses are solicited, a seller is selected and contract awarded.

13: C

Well-developed virtual communication skills will help the most. Without polished skills in this area, use of email and instant messaging may not be effective. Responsibility assignment matrix is helpful in both virtual and co-location settings but may not be fully effective without proper communication. Knowledge of local language and customs will help but cannot be considered the MOST effective of all four.

14: D

Project life cycle differs from industry to industry but product life cycle is the same. Project life cycle produces the product and each type of product requires different life cycle phases to go through. The product life cycle starts with conception of the product idea and ends with termination or retirement of the product. Project life cycle always has a methodology to follow, it may be weak or loosely tied together but it does exist. Product life cycle spans multiple project life cycles not the other way around. Project life cycle output is the product not the project.

15: B

The first thing to do is to provide the completed deliverables to the sponsor/customer and obtain acceptance of those deliverables. Work will stop immediately but you should go through the acceptance of deliverables and Close Project process before releasing resources. Project termination decisions are rarely made because of project team's performance. The biggest reason is misalignment with changed business direction.

16: D

Shipping product order received through internet would be difficult to qualify as a project even though it is a larger order than usual. Shipping orders is a well-defined repeated process. There might be a start but there really is no defined end. It does not end with a unique product and no progressive elaboration is needed. In fact the whole process can be put down as standard operation procedure where each step is well defined.

17: C

A purchase order or invitation to bid is issued during the Conduct Procurement process. The process is completed when the contract is awarded. In this case issuing of purchase order and acceptance by the seller will complete this process.

18: C

Actual Cost (AC) = $300,000

Budget At Completion (BAC) = $400,000

Since project is 75% complete, 75% of $400,000 = $300,000

So Earned Value (EV) = $300,000

19: D

It does not matter if the stakeholders have a negative or positive impact on the project; their needs must be met based on their level of influence, power, and alignment of their interest with the project's objectives.

20: C

In Control Quality process the work itself or attributes of work are measured to compare against the standard set by the quality plan, therefore deliverables are an input to this process. Change requests and validated changes are output of the process. Perform Quality Assurance is a process not an input.

21: A

Since the work was completed as specified and deliverables were provided, the work should be considered complete. The level of customer satisfaction cannot impact the completion and closure of project. It is too late to cancel or put the contract on hold as the work is already complete.

22: C

Project audits, transition criteria, and lessons learned knowledge base all impact the Close Project or Phase process. It is too late for marketplace conditions to have any impact on Close Project or Phase process. This may have an impact in the earlier processes especially on initiation and planning processes.

23: B

Requirements are gathered and documented by the project management team. When decision is made to include or exclude requirements from the scope of the project, the project management team records those decision along with explanation.

24: C

The programmer, the vendor, and the workplace manager are all stakeholders because they influence the project and can be affected by the project. The seller responsible for fixing broken chairs does not influence the project and is not impacted by the project, so not a stakeholder.

25: A

Pareto chart is used for classifying and sorting highest frequency factors. What-If scenario analysis helps in looking at the impact of various options on the results. Fast tracking compresses the schedule. Resource leveling puts the resources to best use. In case of a very expensive resource, you want to minimize the non-productive time of the resources and keep the person fully engaged. By doing resource leveling you will be able to achieve that.

26: B

This is called Gold plating i.e. adding features or functions that are beyond requirements or upgrading a product when it is not required. It may not bring the value but does create risks for the project.

27: A

These changes are uniquely identified and documented using a formal communication which could be formal verbal followed by formal written.

28: B

Project team and project management plan would be developed later after the project charter has been approved. Business case provides the background and objectives of the project but does not describe the culture, policies, procedures, etc. A study and review of enterprise environmental factors that include culture, policies, standards, infrastructure, marketplace conditions, etc. will be the most helpful for you.

29: A

When the project scope is unclear, an iterative approach is really helpful where each phase builds on the results from the previous phase. Sequential relationship and Predictive life cycle will be prone to many errors and rework as the scope becomes clear passing through the phases. There is no such method as intimated relationship.

30: A

There are more channels of communication in a matrix structure than in a functional or a projectized structure. Therefore, the communication will be more complex in a matrix structure. Efficiency of communication depends on how it is managed; it can be low in a simple structure just because it is not being managed well.

31: C

The start-to-start relationship means the second task starts after the start of the first task. Since there is a 5 days lag, the second task will start 5 days after the start of the first task.

32: D

SWOT stands for Strengths, Weaknesses, Opportunities, and Threats. It is a technique used for analyzing risk and understanding its dynamics.

33: C

These will be in the initiating process group. Once planning starts, schedule constraints along with all other constraints are explored and further defined. These are well defined by the time scheduling starts. Scope definition has nothing to do with schedule constraints in general.

34: B

Defining activities, estimating activity resources, and develop schedule is one time effort after that throughout the rest of the project life cycle, the schedule has to be controlled, work performance information has to be made, compared against baselines, reported, if a change occurs then change request has to be processed, approved and then baseline has to be updated. So it is the Control Schedule process that takes most of the effort.

35: C

Gantt chart is used in Develop Schedule process. It represents the work planned over a period of time.

36: A

The project has an approved budget in US dollars but cost of deployment in each country will be different and will be estimated independently. So not only that each country's deployment cost is constrained by the approved budget in US dollars but also the fluctuating currency exchange rate will put a budget constraint on the project. There is no mention of fast track schedule and scope creep. Cost estimation will be independently done for each country but the currency exchange rate will fluctuate this estimation when summed up at the project level. So it is the budget constraint that this scenario is about.

37: C

Creating project scope statement, performing stakeholder analysis, and gathering detailed requirements, all are planning activities. The project has to be initiated which happens with developing project charter and getting it approved.

38: B

Rejecting technique only works when the affected party is not in a position to exploit the rejection or create or increase the negative impact on the project.

Avoidance is a good technique if the problem is expected to go away on its own or is of very low significance.

Compromising is another good technique that works really well in situations where both parties have somewhat equal or powerful impact but this happens with a sacrifice which may not be the best option for the project.

Confronting a problem is the best technique because the focus is on understanding and removing the root cause of the problem. Even if the root cause is not fully removed, the knowledge of its impact is very helpful in managing it.

39: B

The Validate Scope process completes when the deliverables have been accepted by the sponsor/customer. Therefore, acceptance of deliverables must be the main objective of this process. The only feedback that we receive from customer is regarding acceptance or rejection of deliverable and the reason for it. So this is not the correct answer. Though Project or Phase Close process cannot start until Validate Scope process has completed, starting the later phase cannot be the main objective of current phase.

40: A

Among the four choices, meetings is the tool and technique of Plan Scope Management process.

41: D

The project manager should evaluate the impact this request has on the project and if needed make the appropriate changes to the communication management plan. All the other three options require that a proper impact assessment has been done otherwise it will be a step taken in the dark.

42: A

A corrective action is the measure that is implemented to bring future results in line with the project management plan. A change request may be recommending corrective/defect repair or preventive action.

43: D

Work authorization system is used to manage at what time and in what sequence tasks are to be executed/worked on. It does not manage resources, record activity attributes or manage project performance.

44: D

He is following the Halo Effect. Just because the contractor did a really good job with office plumbing project does not mean he is qualified to do work on high pressure gas pipeline project with totally different quality, delivery, and other requirements. So he missed the qualification of the seller. Bidder's conference happens when multiple prospective sellers are involved. The invitation to the seller is the request for proposal, maybe not called as such in this case. Independent estimate is not required. When only one seller is being invited, the buyer is well aware of the costs involved otherwise multiple sellers would have been invited.

45: D

A communication is confirmed to have happened when the encoded message was sent and received and feedback was then sent and received.

Project manager's email of the issue only covers the first half of communication. It does not say if the sponsor received the communication and confirmed.

A minutes of meeting document is the message but was not sent to anyone in this example.

Project progress report in company's newsletter is one way communication. There is no indication that it was read.

Team member's performance improvement is the correct answer because the training (message) was given (sent) to the team member (receiver) who then improved his performance (feedback) after getting back to work.

46: C

The focus of the project manager should be to resolve the issue. Asking team members to ignore it can make it a bigger issue later on since it is still there. Whether the issue is discussed in private or public, it still is an issue between the two members and need a resolution. Change requests are only created for items that are being tracked through configuration management system and need to be modified. The project manager should try to understand what the disagreement is so that he/she can suggest a solution to resolve it.

47: C

Causal/econometric method would be the best because it considers the factors or causes that may affect the forecast and uses regression analysis to understand the impact. In this case collective agreement renewal may impact the future performance of the project so a good understanding of the underlying causes is needed. Performance review and time series methods are based on the past and use that to predict future performance. These methods will not be effective in this scenario. Judgmental methods are based on intuition and opinion and may not uncover the effects of the causes.

48: B

In order to find the root cause of certain issues, fishbone diagramming is a very effective tool. All other three options require that reasons for non-conformances are known before any step can be taken.

49: C

A discussion about performance in the presence of a human resource representative is a verbal discussion in a formal setting. It will be written if the decision or agreement made in the meeting is recorded and distributed. It could have been considered informal if the HR representative was not present and the discussion was more around exploring problems with the team member.

50: C

Recommendations from the quality assurance/audit report can result in change requests. Quality plan and metrics are output of Plan Quality Management process while quality control measurements are output of Control Quality process.

51: B

Customer or sponsor cannot be forced or pressurized to accept deliverables. So asking for help from other stakeholders and forcing acceptance because these are as per plan will not work. If there is a change in business need, appropriate step will be to create a change request so that rejected deliverables could be modified to meet the business need. This holds true if the deliverables can be modified or fixed. If the deliverables do not meet the business need, it is time to review if the project is still valid and whether it should be continued or killed.

52: C

In a Projectized organization, project manager has full control over project resources. In a functional organization, functional manager has full control over resources. In a weak matrix organization, project manager works as a project coordinator or expediter, and does not have control over project resources. His role is to coordinate the work and implement the decisions.

53: C

Organizational process assets include lessons learned databases, risk management templates, and policies and procedures. Policies and procedures cannot be updated through projects though recommendation for an update can be made. So 'lessons learned database and risk management templates' is the correct answer.

54: C

It is the project team working or executing the project that need the list of factors; what will the sponsor and end user do with a list of factors? They would rather see the steps project manager is taking to bring the project back on track. In order to add new activities or redevelop schedule, an approved change request is required. Therefore, a change request to update schedule baseline should be created.

55: B

Project scope management is not about completing on time and within budget though these are the triple constraints, meaning change in one will impact one or both of the other. It is to do with doing all the work required to be done to achieve the project objectives and doing only the required work and no more.

56: D

Sensitivity analysis checks the impact of changing one variable only while all other variables are kept constant. This is done for most variables and at the end the most volatile factors are considered for response planning since they have a chance of a higher impact, if they occur.

57: C

Using data from previous similar projects to come up with cost estimate of a new project is done in the Analogous estimating technique. Ball Park is a high level estimate that mostly takes expert judgment into account.

Bottom up estimating is doing estimation at activity level and then summing it up. Parametric estimating takes historical data and statistical analysis to come up with an estimate.

58: C

This idea is presented by Expectancy theory. McGregor's theory X and Y refer to the perception management holds about the employees but it does not mean they are true to that perception. Maslow's theory presents various levels of motivation based on needs.

59: A

It is clear from the scenario that the project is in a matrix organization. It cannot be a weak matrix organization since the project manager reports to the functional manager so if there is any escalation it will be to the project manager's own functional manager. In strong matrix organization, project manager has enough authority to go to the senior of a functional manager and escalate resource or other problems directly. Therefore this can occur in strong matrix organization.

60: A

Parametric estimating takes historical data and statistical analysis so it is much more accurate than an opinion based on expert judgment. You should use $750,000 estimate.

61: A

Such a method is called Critical Chain Method, where buffers can be introduced in different ways within the project schedule to accommodate for the resource constraint. It adds buffer to manage the uncertainty, which in this scenario is around resource availability.

62: C

Business case for the project cannot have affected the development of the plan because it is not an input to Develop Project Management Plan process. The templates, lessons learned, and change management policies affect the development of the plan.

63: D

All these pieces of information are part of the project management plan. Project charter does not talk about project life cycle selection or results of process tailoring. Risk management plan is focused on risks not life cycle selection. Project life cycle selection directs project schedule.

64: D

The probability of occurrence of a risk or impact if the risk occurs goes up and down during project execution as project's internal and external conditions change. Risks that are close to being one requiring a response can be put on a watch list and monitored so that if their probability of occurrence or impact increases, a response can be planned.

65: A

It means variables are closely related to each other. A change in one variable will result in a change in the other one.

66: A

A Pareto diagram will show the types of issues occurring and their frequency sorted from high to low so that focus can be diverted on the most frequent issues.

67: C

Stakeholders' list is not a work performance data. There is nothing on that list that provides any information related to how work has been performed.

68: D

Analytical techniques is a tool and technique of Plan Schedule Management process. This tool includes scheduling methodology, scheduling techniques, fast tracking and crashing techniques, etc.

69: B

Labor costs, material costs, and equipment costs are all included in the cost baseline but management cost is usually put as an overhead on the project. This means it is a set number or percentage that is booked against the project but does not form part of the cost baseline.

70: A

Since this is a change request, it should be in a formal written communication. Change request will impact project plan and baselines once approved hence they have the potential of affecting the project goals. Being written, formal communication brings clarity and confirms agreement by the parties.

71: C

A portfolio does not have a start and end dates like projects and programs do. Projects and programs get added to the portfolio when these are to be worked on or taken out of the portfolio when these are completed or cancelled. The portfolio continues.

72: D

These are the functions performed by the configuration control and integrated change control system. Control chart has no role in change request processing. There is nothing called configuration chart in this context. Change control board is part of change control but this covers only a portion of the work mentioned in the above scenario.

73: C

If there is an issue with a team member's performance, it will be discussed in private with the relevant manager or leader but definitely not in a status review meeting with executive stakeholders.

74: B

People who will be directly affected by the project are called stakeholders. They are identified and recorded on stakeholder register, which is a list of stakeholders, during the Initiating process group. Although the identification of stakeholders and update of list happens throughout project life cycle, it is the Initiating process group where the list is created.

75: C

The resource cost for additional resources has to come from somewhere. Management reserve is kept specifically for the purpose of unknown risks and unexpected expenses. The scenario does not mention anything about risks occurring so it means this was unexpected. Hence funds should be requested from the management reserve. Purpose of adding more resources is to stay on schedule so there is no reason to modify schedule baseline. No risk has been mentioned so no risk can be closed. There is no change to the scope so no need to review the scope.

76: B

Such a review is called a procurement audit. It is a planned pre-defined process to review the procurement process and its results and understand what went well and what didn't.

77: B

First thing is to find out what is going on. So project manager should review the acceptance criteria, the deliverable and customer's objection as well as team's arguments. Confronting approach is right but without the knowledge it cannot be said that forcing technique should be used. Change request cannot be submitted without knowing what is to change.

78: A

A composite resource calendar shows the competency level, experience level, and availability schedule of a resource but it does not show the hourly rate of that resource.

79: D

Adding scope does not necessarily mean that more risks must be added. Instead risk identification must be performed to identify if there are any new risks.

80: B

Total Quality Management is a business philosophy. The purpose is to find and modify methods that will create a continuous improvement environment for the products, services, and business practices.

81: C

The purpose of phase initiation processes is to keep the project aligned to the business goals and meet the business need. By reviewing project charter and stakeholders list, the project gets realigned to the business. Changes to project charter are rare but this is the perfect time to see that business objectives of the project have changed and require an update to the project charter. Previous phase closure would already have happened that is why new phase is being initiated. Following processes for the purpose of following processes is not a good reason.

82: B

Best option is to hire the team leader's son if he meets all other criteria. If the son meets all criteria but the experienced resource is hired against the country's norms, the project is being setup for problems. The productivity expected from hiring an experienced resource may be totally gone.

Replacing team leader does not change the normal practice. Maybe the new team leader also has a son or daughter or some other relative interested in the job.

Though team leader is responsible for getting the work done, the project manager needs to do the due diligence and make sure whoever is hired has the capability to get the job done since ultimately he/she is responsible for delivering the project.

83: D

Team building activities should not be work related. In most cases it will develop a feeling that the team members are being tricked to do more work in the name of team building and this can be damaging to the team building itself.

84: A

The purpose of a quality audit is to identify what needs to improve and how improvements can be made. It does not pinpoint individual performance or provide material for performance evaluation. Therefore, the best option is to explain to the team that it will benefit the project and the team by identifying which policies and procedures are ineffective and inefficient.

85: C

A notice with such conviction only comes out when there is formal power. Since there is no mention or hint of disciplinary action, it cannot be called coercive power. The power that the senior project manager was asked to display was expert power because of his/her experience. The question is not what senior project manager is displayed but what he referred to.

86: C

A quality audit is an independent review to check the adequacy and efficiency of policies and procedures.

87: C

Assume 'm' is the number of months.
Then, Buy option: \$150,000 + \$5,000 x m.
Rent option: \$5,000 + \$10,000 x m
Solving for m, 150,000 + 5,000 m = 5,000 + 10,000 m
m = 29 months

88: B

Review of individual member's performance, including project manager, is not put on a dashboard so this report does not show performance of project manager vs. other team members or any resource. The question does not mention any rating so it cannot be the choice about seller's performance. Though seller rating is linked to the performance of work, it is not what this report refers to. The report shows schedule, budget, and scope including % complete and status of where actual stands vs. planned. This is a common project status report that gives a good understanding of where the project stands in terms of performance.

89: B

The receiver of the message is the one who decodes the message and so can also be called as decoder. In this case, since project manager received the message, he/she is the decoder. Vendor's representative is the encoder or sender and letter is the medium through which the message has been sent.

90: B

As the project progresses from initiating to planning to executing to closing, the stakeholders' influence keeps reducing. This is because the cost of making a change keeps on increasing as the project progresses. The stage where most of the budget is spent and maximum resources are engaged is the executing stage. The level of influence stakeholders can exert in the executing stage as compared to initiating and planning stage has reduced.

91: C

Expert judgment is what we obtain using these techniques. It can be to create stakeholders' list, collect data for quality assurance, or project progress report.

92: C

Negotiation is the preferred approach because it saves time and money and brings minimum disruption to the project. Court and arbitration takes significantly longer time. Mediation takes more time than negotiation; a third party has to be involved and of course needs to be compensated. So it has both time and cost impact greater than negotiation.

93: C

Having a clear agenda creates a focus in the meeting. Also ground rules help in directing participants' behavior about and during the meeting. A ground rule that whenever there is a discussion we will go around the table and everyone will have a chance to present his/her opinion will not just stop interruptions but also everyone speaking at the same time. This will also encourage participation by all. Advising all in attendance to discuss one topic at a time is a partial solution to the problem. Having established ground rules that have been put in writing accomplishes it better. Number of people and participation is not an issue here.

94: B

Once the costs have been estimated, Determine Budget process aggregates the estimated costs of individual work packages. Total cost of the project is established and budget approval is requested after adding contingency and management reserves to it.

95: B

The purpose of quality assurance is to identify how the whole quality management can be improved end to end so this is a management process.

96: C

Writing performance report of individual resources can be performed anytime during project execution, at the end or afterwards and is totally independent of resource engagement or release from a project.

97: B

A handoff of work from one phase to another will identify the transition. Deliverables could be the one being handed off to the next team but deliverables do not identify transition, these identify completion of work within a phase. Project reports and milestones could show phase end but do not identify phase transition.

98: D

Already approved project budget, in itself, is not considered historical information. It belongs to the current project. All the other three are either direct historical information sources or derived information based on historical data and experience.

99: C

Acceptance of final product by the customer is scope validation so that is not the right choice. The question does not say if it is a contract or not so procurement closure cannot be the choice. Earned value is used for performance evaluation and not needed after completion of work. One of the activities performed during Close Project or Phase process is creation or update of lessons learned document. This is the best choice among the four.

100: B

In order to define scope of a project, requirements should already have been gathered and documented. The requirement documentation becomes an input to Define Scope process. At the start of Define Scope process, requirements traceability matrix contains only the list of gathered requirements and its purpose is to link those requirements to the business needs. Project scope statement is an output of the process while product analysis is a tool and technique.

101: B

Project scope statement will not have the list of activities that must be completed to achieve project's objectives. That list is created from WBS work packages separately during Define Activities process.

102: D

Project team is responsible for the quality of the deliverables, no matter what type of project it is. Seller, sponsor, QA team can play a secondary role but they are not responsible.

103: A

Customers do not view project life cycle as product life cycle. Project life cycle is a subset of product life cycle in that several project life cycles may occur in a product life cycle. A project life cycle ends with delivering the product while a product life cycle ends with retiring the product.

104: C

The Projectized organizational structure is built with project team reporting directly to the project manager in the hierarchy of the organization. There is no functional manager role in a Projectized structure. Each team member will have one reporting line and that is to his/her project manager. Team members may or may not be co-located just like in a functional organization.

105: C

First time analysis would fall under planning but since risk identification and analysis is a continuous process, Control Risks process takes care of identification of more risks, analysis of new risks and re-analysis of changed risks.

106: B

Contractual provisions are terms and conditions of the contract but for the buyer these would become constraints as these put limitations on the project. Provisions or terms and conditions are for the supplier's work. Contractual provisions cannot be considered changes or risks but those two can occur because of the constraints.

107: C

Risk identification is a continuous process throughout project life cycle. If a risk is identified, no matter by whom, it should be recorded on the risk register and analyzed. If it requires a response, then a response should be prepared.

108: D

The activities mentioned in the scenario are all Control Risks process activities. Therefore, they are part of the Monitor and Control Project Work process.

109: A

This process is performed at each phase end. It helps in ensuring that work in one phase was completed and accepted before moving to the next phase.

110: A

Control charts do not show relationships between two factors. Scatter diagram can be used to see relationship between two factors.

111: A

The purpose of the project charter is to authorize the project manager to proceed with the project therefore the project charter gives more authority to the project manager. Business case has already been created and is an input to develop project charter process. Creating project charter helps to get approval of project charter otherwise there is nothing to be approved. This is not a reasonable answer. Creating project charter helps with stakeholder identification indirectly and is not the main purpose or benefit of it.

112: D

Apply approved changes to the baseline schedule happens in Direct and Manage Project Work process. Though all the other three are objectives of schedule control process, the controlling of changes encompasses the other two and is the main objective.

113: B

Preferential or discretionary activities can create arbitrary float values and if not fully documented will make it difficult to modify the schedule.

114: A

Using current rate of progress is incorrect because resource shortage issue is gone which had affected current performance. A totally new estimate will be a wasted effort since whatever has been the main reason affecting performance has been fixed. Current rate of progress for design work cannot be used as the resource is available now. Therefore, the best choice is to use original planned rate of progress to calculate estimate to complete.

115: D

Quality and grade are often taken one and the same but these are two different terms. Quality is that feature is meeting specifications while grade is that there are more features.

116: B

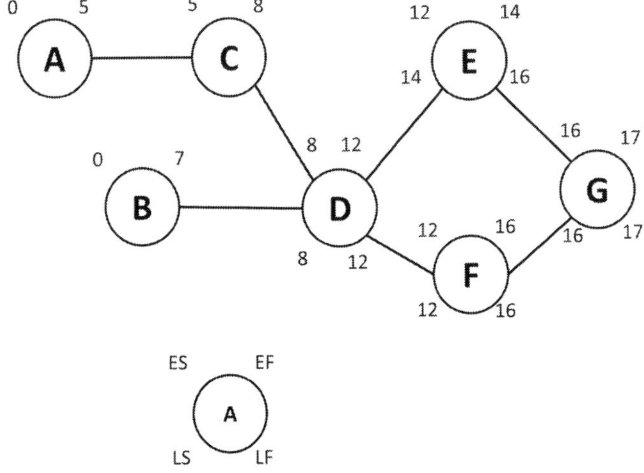

On the backward pass, when the network is converging, the lesser of all the converging activities is the Late Finish date of the converged activity. In this case, 14 and 12 are Late Start dates of activity E and F respectively, taking the lesser one, 12 is the Late Finish date of activity D.

117: A

Resource calendars do not contain location and contact information of resources. Those pieces of information are kept on team roster.

118: A

The purpose of Direct and Manage Project Work process is to get the work done, the result of which are the deliverables. Therefore, deliverables among the four choices is an output of the process. Project charter is output of Develop Project Charter process. Project Management Plan is an output of Develop Project Management Plan process. Project forecasts are output of Monitoring and Controlling Project Work process.

119: B

WBS does not have any information related to project objectives. Actually a project objective is what drives the development of WBS but does not show on the WBS.

120: B

Review of individual team member's performance on the project is what is being considered in project performance appraisals. Individual's performance does affect overall performance of the project in general but overall project performance is not considered an individual's performance. 3rd party project appraisals or audit are focused on project performance not individual performance.

121: B

Although documenting each stakeholder's requirements is a good idea, ranking them in terms of favorability to the project will only create friction among various stakeholders. Only stakeholders who are not impacted by the project and cannot influence the project should be removed from stakeholders list. Sponsor can help in classifying stakeholders but cannot advise in concrete terms as to who should be taken care of more than others. It is the project manager's responsibility to understand the impact and influence and manage them accordingly.

The best option is to use focus groups and brainstorming sessions and encourage objectives discussion among stakeholders to reach a common ground and define clear non-competing objectives.

122: B

Identifying stakeholder throughout the project life cycle cannot be effectively done by the project manager alone. Project team members should be on the lookout and identify if they find someone who is being impacted by the project or can influence the project.

123: A

Quality is not meeting scope but the needs, even if these are not implied. For example, a seller building a house that is not habitable is not meeting quality. Even if the contract does not say the house has to be habitable, the need of it to be habitable is implied and cannot be ignored.

124: D

Since you are having challenges with project B, you need to find out what challenges were faced by the previous project and how were those handled. So you should do a review of project documentation and lessons learned of that project and also speak to its project manager, if possible.

The issue is not that you cannot manage two projects at the same time but you are having problems controlling one project. So putting one project on hold or not starting another project, both are not the right answers.

Scope control is as much required as cost, schedule or quality control on a project. There is a difference in defining requirements completely and expanding scope. Scope should be baselined and then the requirements defined completely.

125: B

WBS does not contain the list of project activities but only work packages through decomposition. WBS is not used to distribute work to project resources though it decomposes work to work package level after which activities can be created, estimated and resources assigned. Also WBS does not contain list of project deliverables but that the project deliverables somewhat drives how the WBS is structured. WBS is the work decomposed hierarchically to the work package level which can then be further decomposed into activities and assigned to teams and individuals.

126: D

PERT analysis and Monte Carlo simulation are used for estimation, while earned value technique is used for performance evaluation. So you will use expert judgment to determine which change requests should be approved.

127: A

Independent estimates provide a cost estimate that can be used to compare prospective sellers' cost estimate. Since it is independent it is expected to be free from bias one way or another.

128: D

Since no resources are available, the schedule cannot be crashed but the review has shown that most dependencies built between activities are discretionary and not mandatory so it means that the schedule can be fast tracked by changing the schedule to perform activities in parallel. Fast tracking would be the best option. Removing non-critical activities will not affect the schedule end date since the end date is driven by the critical activities. It does not make sense to define activities as non-important and major.

129: B

Optimistic estimate = 4 hours
Pessimistic estimate = 12 hours
Most Likely estimate = 10 hours
PERT formula is (O + 4M + P) / 6 = (4 + 4x10 + 12) / 6 = ~9 hours

130: C

Appropriate processes and the level of implementation should be selected to meet project objectives so that it is neither too little processes that project could not be managed effectively nor too many that project manager and team spends unnecessary time on project management activities that do not add value to the project. Project manager alone should not make the decision. He/she should involve stakeholders to come up with an appropriate level of rigor for the project.

131: D

What is it that the experts provide and non-experts do not? Expert Judgment. Scenario is directed toward clearing the audit, it means the project is wrapping up and your concern is to close the project really well so that no issues come up when audited. Scope validation is not in question. Enterprise environmental factors and organizational process assets are not tools but input/output to a process.

132: D

Reserve analysis is a tool used during Control Costs process and is not an input to determine project budget (a planning process).

133: D

In a functional organization, all work is assigned by the functional manager. Sponsor or project team members do not have the authority to assign work. Project manager assigns work in Projectized organization. In strong matrix organizations, project manager may assign work based on how much time a resource has been allocated to the project by the functional manager.

134: C

Cost plus material fee does not make sense as material is already a cost that is being reimbursed under the term 'cost'. All other three are valid cost-reimbursable contracts.

135: A

It is the project manager's responsibility to manage the project, create the status report, and provide the status report to the appropriate stakeholders. Therefore, sponsor does not lead project status review meetings, project manager does.

136: A

Risk register contains all the identified risks but the project charter has a high level view of the risks. Risk management plan is part of the project management plan and it does not contain a list of risks.

137: D

Whenever there is a change in a project life cycle, it usually impacts scope, time and/or cost. The result is that baselines get impacted and need to be updated. In other words, re-planning happens frequently when there are too many changes. If changes are passed through integrated change control system, properly evaluated, approved and then implemented, these should not impact team morale. It is the unplanned and unevaluated changes that start to give the feeling of lost control and that is when team morale and stakeholder satisfaction will get impacted. With approved changes, project targets also get aligned so meeting of project targets is not an issue.

138: B

Your biggest concern should be that how is your project being impacted by this change. You need to understand the impact before deciding that you have to hire an external resource. First come first serve is not the principle used when making business decisions. After you have understood impact, you should inform management how your project is getting impacted and request for the resource's reassignment to your project. Compress schedule will not result in anything except increasing risks for the project.

139: B

The developer making a change or adding new information to the report without any prior approval or discussion is an example of scope creep. Scope creep can happen for any reason, one of which is, when the team starts adding minor things into the scope because they feel it is not taking any extra time or money. Adding scope without approval is a very risky approach to exceed expectations and is not recommended.

140: A

More than 50 percent of the message is nonverbal in face-to-face communication. Different face expressions and hand gestures can change the meaning of what is being said in the mind of the receiver.

141: B

Advertising as a tool is used in Conduct Procurements process where responses are solicited from sellers interested in bidding for the contract.

142: B

Work Performance Data is an input to the Control Communications process which is then analyzed and results in Work Performance Information as an output.

143: B

An approved change request due to change in the price of drill bits is a good reason to update project performance baselines. Adding more resources to the project on fixed price contract will not need a change request. Rework by supplier to fix a defect usually will not be accommodated with a change request, at least from cost perspective. Buying a new machine by a contractor is his cost and should not generally impact the project baselines.

144: A

The issues being faced by the project manager show that meetings are not in control or it could be that the team members are not really sure what they are doing there. Best approach is to set ground rules for the meeting. For example, inform the project manager if you are late or going to be absent, don't leave the room in the middle without letting know, no calls or texting during the meeting, etc.

145: D

A contract can be completed or can be terminated or cancelled before completion. Closing a contract requires that the contract either be completed or terminated/cancelled.

146: A

Since he is highly interested he should be kept informed on project progress and because he is an expert in domain knowledge, he should be solicited for opinion and feedback on estimation, planning, risks and issues. Due to low influence this stakeholder does not need to be managed closely. Sending regular project reports only will satisfy his high interest but will not benefit the project.

147: D

Configuration management system contains the list of all items that are under change control so if there is any change to any of those items; this system provides how the change is to be made including the process of going through the change and updating the item.

148: D

Work is produced in Direct and Manage Project Work process while work and project performance is reviewed in the Monitor and Control Project Work process.

149: D

First identify the main stakeholders which will include the sponsor, heads of the department affected by the project, project team, project management office, etc. Then expand that list by speaking with the identified main stakeholders and continue this while developing project charter. As you dig deeper into the project you will unearth more stakeholders. Salience model and stakeholder matrix will analyze stakeholders not identify them. Identify all stakeholders is the challenge. The question is asking how.

150: B

The purpose of resource histogram is to see how much work has been assigned to the resource over a period of time. Since assigning of work to resources is part of planning, resource histograms are created in the Plan Human Resource Management process.

151: B

A project manager is focused on the project goals and hence will take steps that move him/her closer to achieving those goals. Sending an apology note or doing a performance review first does not help with the objectives. Increasing project communication does not solve the problem, viz. not regularly updating the issue log. Sponsor is worried seeing issues have stayed opened for long time so project manager should review those open issues, get them updated and resolved.

152: B

After quantitative risk analysis is completed, risks are prioritized and top priority risks are reviewed for response planning. Risk register is continuously updated not just after quantitative risk analysis rather throughout the project. Though this answer is correct too but the better answer is 'prioritization is done.'

153: A

The project manager should review the requirements and figure out with the team how to fix or recreate the deliverable. As per contract, project team has to complete the deliverable that satisfies the acceptance criteria. Finger pointing at who is responsible for failed deliverable will just result in wastage of time. There is no need to review the referred term if the project manager already agrees with buyer's interpretation. Change request, if needed, will come after appropriate course of action has been selected.

154: B

Fire and theft, injury and life risks all have a negative outcome. Only business risks are one, in this list, that can have a positive or a negative outcome. So the focus is to plan for the risk in such a way that a negative outcome can be converted into a positive one, if possible.

155: D

Fixed price or lump sum contract is most commonly used when the product specifications are well defined and detailed. Time and material is commonly used when total scope is undefined but have a good idea which direction to proceed. Time lapsed would be a time and material contract, if defined as a contract. In cost reimbursable contracts, the risk is mostly taken by the buyer. These types of contracts are hard to establish with ambiguous specifications.

156: A

If contingency reserve is added or included as part of cost, it bloats the estimate and does not give the true picture. It will also make it difficult to get the budget approved. Further, it also loosens project manager's control over project costs as the cost performance baseline is not correct.

157: C

Change log is the only input, among the four choices, to Manage Stakeholder Engagement. Among various plans, only Stakeholder Management Plan and Communications Management Plan are the input.

158: C

Handover the final product of the project to the customer happens in Validate Scope process. This starts the Project Close process.

159: C

This document is called lessons learned document and it is created in the Closing process. The document becomes an organizational process asset and can be used as an input in later phases or future projects.

160: D

Cost performance baseline is not derived from schedule performance baseline. Though both seem to go hand in hand, they are separate in essence.

161: C

Pitch and tone of the voice and body language is the most important to understand argument. Meanings of same sentence change dramatically with the change in pitch, tone and body language. The subject matter expertise, if brought into as a guide to understand the arguments, actually is a bias that stops the listener from understanding the argument. Facts and fiction do help understand argument but it's the pitch, tone and body language that gives them the meaning. Time of day has no bearing on the understanding.

162: B

Procurement specialist will take the lead role because they are trained and experienced in ensuring a good outcome for both parties.

163: B

Gathering requirements is not a part of the kickoff activity. In fact it should never be used to gather requirements. The purpose of kickoff meeting is to introduce the project team, get stakeholders involved and excited about the project, and make the roles and responsibilities clear to all the stakeholders.

164: B

There are two techniques that can be used to compress a schedule. Fast tracking and crashing. Fast tracking is done by running activities in parallel and crashing schedule is done by adding more resources so that work can be completed earlier. Since the scope cannot be reduced, crashing is the technique to be used by engaging more resources. Analyzing and forecasting schedule does not compress the schedule but only provide a picture of how the project is doing.

165: C

Scope baseline is an input to the Perform Qualitative Risk Analysis process. Work breakdown structure is part of the scope baseline along with WBS dictionary and scope statement.

166: D

Variance analysis is performed in the Monitoring and Controlling Project Work process.

167: A

PDM shows the relationship or dependencies between various activities in a graphical format which is not evident in other types of network techniques. PDM does not show progress at any point in time. Whether it is most commonly used or not is not an advantage or disadvantage so this answer is incorrect.

168: C

Management skills are one of the tools and techniques of Manage stakeholder Engagement. WBS defines how the work is structured and so does not play any role in managing stakeholder engagement. RACI chart defines roles and responsibilities but does not impact how stakeholder should be managed. Issue log is an input to the process because in order to resolve issues communication needs to happen, a common understanding between various stakeholders has to be developed.

169: A

Project management information system may record or provide some data but does not play the main role in this process. Procurement audits only provide feedback on how well the procurement process went. Administrative procedures ensure identified process is followed to close the project. Expert judgment helps in ensuring appropriate standards are followed well. The purpose of this process is to ensure all necessary activities to satisfy completion criteria, transfer project's artifacts, perform lessons learned and audit, are performed in an efficient and productive manner.

170: C

Least flexible activities in a schedule are the activities on the critical path. Actually these are non-flexible activities because any change in these activities will change the end date of the schedule. Therefore, you are using the critical path method. PDM in itself does not show flexibility of activities without critical path information. It shows the relationship between activities. PERT analysis uses three estimates to find the duration of each activity and does not show which activities are least flexible.

171: C

There is no response planning being done. Risks have already been identified. Risk analysis is being done but it is a process not a technique. The only technique in the four choices is Delphi technique, which uses multiple respondents anonymously for finding out opinions.

172: A

Project charter is not an input, output or tool and technique of Direct and Manage Project Work process. All others are one of those.

173: D

WBS dictionary is a document that provides detailed information surrounding a WBS item or work package. Among several other pieces of information, it contains the cost estimates, resources required, and account codes. So WBS dictionary will help the project accountant identify the cost center of that resource.

174: D

Risk score is calculated by multiplying probability of occurrence with the impact. If the probability of occurrence is very high and the risk score is low it means the impact is very low. Same will be the case when probability of occurrence is very low and impact is very high, it will result in low risk score.

175: B

List of identified risks is just one piece of information on the risk register. There is no concept of check-in check-out risks. Not all risks require responses only the one that are significant, need to have a response planned. It is a document that contains all of the outcomes of risk management process including analysis, response planning, watch lists, expected monetary value, etc.

176: C

The Salience model classifies stakeholders on the basis of their power, urgency, and legitimacy.

177: D

If the project has been cancelled, Close Project process starts to close the project. If the sponsor stops the support, project is kind of abandoned, so Close Project process kicks in. If project plan gets rejected, this means project cannot proceed so Close Project process starts to end the project. A late project does not mean project has been cancelled, abandoned, or completed; steps have to be taken to improve performance. The Project Close process does not start.

178: D

Stakeholder register is an input to Plan Quality Management process because it identifies stakeholders with an interest in the quality and influence on project quality standards.

179: D

Among the four choices only network diagram shows the longest time between planned start and finish dates. It shows various routes from start to finish date and the longest one can be determined from among all the routes shown.

180: D

If the project budget is affected, then the project's cost performance baseline needs to be updated after the change is approved. Earned value is the work completed so it does not get affected by an approved change to project's budget. Integrated change control system does not need any update. Project charter seldom gets updated but if it does then it is because the project objectives have significantly changed.

181: B

A corrective action is a type of change request. When we are thinking about risk response and we bring in corrective action then it is the change that we need to put in place to handle the risk. In other words, putting the planned risk response into action is a corrective action. A corrective action will be taken if a risk occurs while a preventive action, in most cases, will happen before the risk occurs so that either its chance of occurrence or impact can be reduced.

182: C

It is not brainstorming, decision making, or change control. Since the project manager is reviewing the large number of errors and trying to see what are root causes of that, he is performing quality assurance where root causes are identified by not just looking at quality control measurements but also quality plan, policies and procedures.

183: C

Forecasting methods is not a tool or technique used in Control Communications process.

184: D

Project management plan is neither an input nor an output of the Develop Project Charter process. A project charter is an output of the process which then becomes input to the Develop Project Management Plan process. 'Statement of work' and 'business need' are input to Develop Project Charter process.

185: D

Deliverables that have been accepted become the input to the Closing process group. Since work is complete, change request and quality control measurements cannot be an input to the Closing process group which happens after completion of work. Though there could be a phase end or project end performance report created, it is not needed in the Closing process.

186: B

Mediation is an Alternative Dispute Resolution (ADR) technique where a 3rd party is involved to listen to arguments from both sides and help them reach an agreement. The other three are not dispute resolution techniques.

187: B

Procurements have to be closed before the project can be closed though in some cases contract will continue from one phase to another. Both Close Project or Phase and Close Procurements involve the customer or sponsor. The Close Procurements process does not require return of all property but it may require return of certain property as already defined in the procurement plan. Close Procurements cannot be repeated for each phase under the same contract.

188: C

Conducting procurement is part of the Executing process group. Controlling Procurements happens after Conduct Procurement is completed and is part of the Monitoring and Controlling process group. Planning happens before procurements are conducted.

189: C

It is a philosophy that improvement to a system, process, etc. must occur on a continuous basis i.e. it is all about continuous improvement.

190: C

In terms of schedule performance, Schedule Variance (SV) is the difference between Earned Value (EV) and Planned Value (PV).

SV = EV - PV = 127,200 - 143,000 = - 15,800 (negative value means behind schedule)

The Schedule Performance Index (SPI) = EV / PV = 127200/143000 = 0.89 which is less than 1, hence project is behind schedule.

191: D

Hiring a truck to move material closer to the site cannot be called cost of quality unless the moving closer to site is to improve or sustain the quality of the material.

192: C

Once change requests are approved, the performance baselines are updated and plans are revised. Without doing that, the project team has no idea how they are supposed to continue the work. Informing project team that the change requests have been approved does not add any value before updating the baselines and the plans. Change requests can only be implemented once they have been included in the plans.

193: C

Source selection happens in the Conduct Procurements process. Once the seller is selected and the contract is awarded, this process is complete.

194: B

The store department objection was that the work packages were too high level, so using analogous and then parametric technique for estimation does not address their objection. Work packaging by type of resources rather than by department will be a difficult approach as work usually cannot be isolated by resources throughout the project and moves between various resources. In this scenario, several departments are involved and it is reasonable to assume that work between departments overlap. So this is not a good approach. By doing a rolling wave planning, work packages do not need to be defined in detail now but later as the work gets closer and requirements and scope gets clearer. This would be a good technique to alleviate store department's concern and help in good estimation when the time arrives.

195: A

Though lessons learned are generally considered as Project or Phase Close activity, lessons learned should be identified throughout the project life cycle. The formal activity ensures these get recorded and reviewed by the team before putting it as a record. Though it is good to have all the stakeholders present, it may not be possible to have them all together frequently, it may be a too large a group, and it may be intimidating for few resources to be open about lessons learned.

196: A

You will explain that there is a cost of quality; it can be cost of conformance or cost of nonconformance. That is, either preventive measures are taken to produce quality product or corrective measures are taken to fix defects in quality.

197: C

Project plan is used to direct the execution of the project, to perform the actual work and produce deliverables while project baseline is used for measuring performance by comparing the actual results with the baselines. Neither project plan nor project baselines change without approved change requests and these are not the same thing.

198: C

Control charts evaluate the past performance and do not predict future or even hint at that. They plot measurements against time to see if these were within limits or not. So control chart is not a forecasting method.

199: C

Stakeholders can be classified as internal and external since both have different kind of influence and needs from the project and can be satisfied with different types of communications. They can be classified as supporter, neutral, and resistor to understand their power, and influence on the project and plan better strategy. Same way high, medium and low influence categorization works well. Identifying stakeholders as executives, managers, and staff does not provide any leverage to the project manager and, in reality, could be detrimental to the project as the focus shifts to satisfying executive stakeholders and ignoring the staff.

200: A

Risk identification happens throughout the project but a good practice is to setup regular reviews periodically to review current risks and identify new risks or analyze new identified risks. For example, for a yearlong project, a monthly review can be a good practice or even a semi-monthly if it is expected that risks will change.

7 - ANSWERS & EXPLANATIONS TEST 3

1: C

Contract change control system cannot be defined separately from the terms of the contract. If it is separate then it will not be part of the contract and unenforceable by the contract.

2: D

Project Management Office does not gather detailed requirements, create project charter or develop project management plan for a project. All these are done by the project manager and the project team.

3: D

Expert judgment is not a technique used in Control Schedule process.

4: A

Once a defect has been repaired it should be reviewed to verify that the defect has been repaired as required. Stakeholders' satisfaction though should be important is not something against which the 'defect repair' will be compared. Project charter only gives a high level of scope. Use of Pareto chart is invalid in this situation.

5: C

Project management process groups are repeated in project phases. So a design phase will be initiated, planned, executed, controlled and closed. Then a construct phase will be initiated, planned, executed, controlled, and closed.

6: C

Since project sponsor is high on both power and interest he/she should be managed closely.

7: D

Organizational Process Assets are the only input to the Develop Project Charter process. All other choices are created much later in the project.

8: D

The correct choice is "A message is encoded by sender, and then sent to the receiver who decodes the message in the presence of some noise." All other options do not present the right sequence and/or process.

9: B

In a Projectized organization, the project manager role is called 'Project Manager'. This type of organization provides maximum authority to the project manager. The project coordinator, facilitator, and expediter are roles with much less authority.

10: D

You should compare the performance baselines with the work performance information and calculate variances. This will lead to forecasting the remaining part of the project. Then you can identify areas of improvement and create corrective actions and also send information to the project sponsor.

11: B

In order to have a better control on the time and material contract, a maximum amount and time limit should be put in the contract. If that was the case, there would not have been such an overrun assuming the limits were below 18 months and $250,000.

12: A

When the project is behind schedule, the Schedule Variance (SV) is negative i.e. Schedule Performance Index (SPI) will be less than 1. Since SPI = EV/PV, it means Earned Value (EV) is less than the Planned Value (PV).

13: B

He used earned value to calculate how much over budget the project will run. But in order to use earned value he had to decide how he is going to forecast. He knew current trend from earned value but now uses his knowledge that the current trend will continue and so forecasted based on his knowledge. There is no use of interpersonal skills or problem solving in this scenario.

14: D

Corrective and preventive actions are not processes. Integrated change control process (which is part of the monitoring and controlling process) will be used if a change has been identified. In this case, monitoring and controlling process will be used to review the work package and proceed with integrated change management if a change is needed.

15: A

Work performance data does not exist when Plan Procurement Management process is being conducted. It is an input to the Control Procurements process.

16: D

An electronic mail does not follow any specific pattern and can be for variety of reasons. It is written in an informal manner.

17: B

Though all the four choices have a component of benefits realization as part of measuring their success, it is the portfolios whose success mainly comes from benefits realization.

18: D

Comparing sample results and measurements with the standards is part of the Control Quality process.

19: B

Buyer is to provide a written notice to the seller that all the work has been completed and all the deliverables have been accepted. This is an output of the Close Procurements process. The other three options can be provided to the seller by the buyer but are not required for the process.

20: C

Project team members are acquired/engaged and developed during execution of the project or phase. Therefore you are in Executing Process Group.

21: A

In the project world, in general, conflicts should be resolved in private. This increases the chance of getting to a resolution faster, parties will be more willing to compromise, and it will be cost effective.

22: C

They may or may not provide work performance data and deliverable status when these are assigned to them. But the reason for these resources to get involved in the project is because of their expertise and therefore all of them provide expert judgment.

23: D

At this stage, he can only provide a ball-park estimate, also known as rough order magnitude estimate. It is a very high level and rough estimate. At the project charter level, he will be able to provide an analogous estimate. Parametric and bottom-up estimates are pretty accurate estimates compared to the above two.

24: C

It is work performance data that is the input to Control Stakeholder Engagement process. Work performance information is the output of this process.

25: C

Stakeholder analysis matrix represents the stakeholder management strategy. Stakeholder register contains the list of identified stakeholders and their interest and influence on the project as well as their role.

26: C

If there are any updates to the project management plan then these will originate from Direct and Manage Project Work and will be an input to the Develop Project Management Plan process so that the project management plan gets updated.

27: C

Control Communications process does not include identification of new stakeholders. All the other three are objectives of it.

28: C

Pareto chart is not used for risk identification. It is a tool to classify various factors and identify the ones that are most frequent. It is used for managing issues rather than managing risk.

29: B

Fishbone diagram is also known as Ishikawa diagram or Cause-Effect diagram.

30: B

Change log is the input to the Manage Stakeholder Engagement process. Issue log and the change request are the output of the process. Work performance data is neither an input nor an output of the process.

31: A

Late start and late finish dates of an activity can be calculated by using the backward pass while going through critical path analysis of the network diagram.

32: C

Division of a large project into phases usually happens at the project charter stage, which is in the Initiating process group. Sometimes this decision may even get delayed till planning stage.

33: A

Expert judgment is a tool and technique not an input to the project management plan.

34: D

To Complete Performance Index describes how the rest of the work needs to be done to meet the originally planned target date and budget. So a TCPI above 1 means performance needs to improve, in this case, 10% above the originally planned performance.

35: A

Global project with team members in different continents is a constraint on project communication. Language and working time are two reasons for that.

36: D

Management style of individual managers is not affected by the culture but by their own experiences and interpersonal skills. All other three are the result of combination of organizational culture and styles.

37: B

Since your manager has refused you resources, it means the resources and you both work for the same manager. This is a characteristic of functional organization. If the resources were coming from different managers it would have been a matrix organization.

38: D

A status report only provides the status of the project at a given time while progress report is a management report that not only provides status report but also gives analysis results and forecast in addition to issues and risks that require actions by the management. Therefore, progress report will be most helpful in understanding the status of the project. Work performance data is raw data and may not be of much worth without analysis against the baselines leading to forecast.

39: A

There are no techniques used in project management for conflict resolution called as schmoozing, flattering, and ignoring. The only valid choice among the four options is compromising, accommodating, collaborating, and forcing.

40: B

Upgrade of the application every two to three years seems like an operational activity but it is in fact a project. The reason is that,

1) Each upgrade will have a definite start and end
2) Each upgrade will result in a unique product (new features, functionality, security, etc.)
3) Each upgrade will use progressive elaboration since there will be new challenges as technology will have changed in 2 to 3 years.

41: B

Risk value is determined by multiplying the probability of a risk with the impact if the risk occurred. The risk value obtained is the risk rating of that risk.

42: C

Out of the four choices, staff compensation should not be of concern in general for the project manager in all types of organization except Projectized. Even in Projectized organization, staff compensation will be managed no differently whether global project or not.

43: C

Since not all identified risks are response planned so risk audit does not look at all identified risks to check if these were planned or not.

44: A

It will be called scope validation in both cases. Phase gate is the process to ensure that one phase has ended so that the next phase may start.

45: D

Cost Variance (CV) = Earned Value (EV) - Actual Cost (AC)

Cost Performance Index (CPI) = EV /AC

If AC is more than EV, it will result in negative cost variance and less than one CPI. Therefore, the project will be over budget.

46: A

The scenario talks about agreement around a discussion. The body language acknowledges that the team member disagrees with the project manager's proposal. 'Transmission' of the message has occurred but this is not the best answer. There is no negotiation and distribution.

47: B

Quality checklist is the best tool among the four choices given. It lists all steps to be performed in sequence which can be followed by different teams and individuals working in different areas. Quality management plan is a weak choice.

48: A

The probability is 70% and the impact to the schedule is 10%. So, 0.7 x 0.1 = 0.07 is the value of risk.

49: C

As a project manager of a project in execution, all you are concerned with is if the new project will have any impact on your project. If you are not assigned to the new project, you cannot initiate the project with a project charter. Leveling resources has no connection with minimizing resource impact without knowing what the impact is. Same way fast tracking project is of no value without understanding the impact first.

50: D

Stakeholders have the most impact at the start of the project because at that time the direction of the project, the requirements and the deliverables, and all other attributes are being set. Any change or addition at this stage has minimum impact on the project's cost and time and thus it is easier to make such changes.

51: D

Statement of work is not a high level, brief document that helps in negotiations and modifications during contract administration. It is a fully detailed scope of work identifying what needs to be accomplished by the seller.

52: D

Risk ranking is an output of the Qualitative Risk Analysis process when the probability and impact have been assigned and multiplied to get the risk value which then helps with risk ranking.

53: C

It cannot be said that internal team's estimate must be incorrect. It may or may not be correct but from the scenario it does not seem to be the issue.

54: B

It is the work breakdown structure components. Though deliverables also represent verifiable products, services or results, but this is a weak choice. The reason is that WBS components encompass all deliverables and has multi-level details so you can have deliverables, work packages, and WBS components under one planning package.

55: A

This is an example of statistical sampling where a few random tests or samples are taken and compared against the standard. The result of this sampling is taken as the result for the population. For example, if 100 random calls were made, and 90 of those say they received the flyer then it's assumed that 90,000 out of 100,000 households received the flyer.

56: C

Expert judgment is the tool and technique which is common to all project integration management processes and rightly so because project integration management is all about integrating all other project management knowledge area processes.

57: B

Project scope statement does not contain work packages; it is the work breakdown structure that contains the work packages.

58: B

Best use of lessons learned is for future projects which use these as historical data for various purposes including estimation, understanding project constraints, assumptions, etc.

59: B

Maslow's theory is irrelevant since it does not address management styles. Theory Z gives employees more freedom and variety of tasks and is more concerned with culture of the organization than the employees. Theory Y gives employees room for creativity and self-management. It is based on macro-management. Theory X management style is based on the assumptions that employees generally dislike work and they need micro-management and strict instructions. This is the correct choice.

60: D

Workarounds are identified in the Control Risks process. It includes choosing an alternative strategy, adopting a workaround, taking a corrective action and implementing a backup plan.

61: D

Resource leveling is not concerned with the skill level of the resources. In other words, skill level of a resource does not play any role in leveling that resource.

62: D

A change request to update performance baselines is the best answer because not only the extra cost needs to be added to the project cost but also the additional scope to the project scope.

63: A

Qualified sellers list is used in Conduct Procurements process. The list contains names of sellers who are qualified to do the work and are invited during this process to bid for the contract.

64: A

Work performance reports is an input to the Manage Communications process. All others are tools and techniques used in this process.

65: C

Evaluate program and project proposal to derive maximum value out of investment is the main goal of portfolio management. The focus on creating a balanced portfolio helps in achieving this objective. All other are the responsibilities of project management office.

66: A

He forced the decision instead of using other techniques. If he had listened to both arguments, understood the root cause and then provided a solution, that would have been problem solving. If the decision was made taking some of each person's argument, it would be called compromising.

67: D

It will result in initiating a project. It may also result in hiring a project manager but not always. The purpose of hiring the project manager will be to initiate the project. Engaging stakeholder may happen for any other reason in addition to the above reason. In this case, it will only happen when a project has been initiated.

68: A

Decision tree does not provide any help in identifying hidden risks. It is concerned with decision making and helps in analyzing various decision options and calculating expected monetary value.

69: A

Project sponsor is the one who authorizes project or phase closure. Remember it is the sponsor who authorizes the project, in the first place, by signing the project charter.

70: C

Once WBS is completed to the work package level, then activities will be defined, after that these will be sequenced then the durations will be estimated. So it is too early to talk about estimating durations.

71: D

A job description only describes what work is to be performed by the resource. A roles and responsibilities document provides detail of what the resource is responsible for and what role the resource will play on the project.

72: C

Executing takes the most time because this is the process group where the action happens. Work is performed, deliverables are created, project team is managed, stakeholders are managed, and procurements are conducted: all in this group.

73: A

Parametric estimation uses statistical relationship between historical data and other factors to come up with an estimate. So $300 per day for expert resource would be the use of parametric estimating. Project cost summed up from each activity's estimate is bottom-up estimating. Project cost distributed down to each activity is top-down estimating. Lessons learned from a previous project is analogous estimating.

74: B

Pareto chart is not used as a tool for Control Schedule process. It is used in quality management processes.

75: A

Informing stakeholder that the information is being sent as per communication plan does not resolve the complaint so this is not a good choice. Asking stakeholder to review the documentation in the project repository is like asking a customer to a bookstore looking for a specific book to go and find it among thousands of books in the store. Reviewing stakeholder's information needs is the right step followed by updating the project communication management plan, if needed. Just sending the plan for review does not do any good.

76: A

Schedule Performance Index (SPI) = 1.06 and Schedule Variance (SV) = $10,000 only tells us that we are ahead of schedule but does not give us the complete picture. We need to know the planned cost, actual cost, and earned value to calculate what is being asked by the finance representative.

77: C

Actual project results or work performance data compared with planned results or performance baselines is called variance analysis and results in variances. Therefore, variance report is what a project manager should use in this situation.

78: B

Risk breakdown structure is not an output of the Control Risks process and so is not an update to the risk register. All the other three choices are an update to the risk register.

79: D

'Analyze communication requirements of stakeholders' is not a part of stakeholder analysis. This will be done as part of developing the communication management plan.

80: D

If a deliverable including final deliverable gets rejected, it needs to be fixed or re-created. This is part of the Validate Scope process, one output of which is, change request. So this is not part of the closing process group.

81: B

Formal acceptance of the completed deliverables is an output of the scope validation process.

82: D

Gate review, kill point, and phase exit are commonly used names for this review but kill review is not a name that is known to be used.

83: D

Business case is the only project document that contains the cost-benefit analysis. Business need is well explained in business case but is referred to in project charter usually. Statement of work and project management plan do not contain both pieces of information.

84: C

Tailoring of processes occur in the planning phase but at the end of the project, you need to see if the tailoring done had any impact on the project, positive or negative. For example, tailoring the process may have saved time on the project because you did not have to go through unnecessary paperwork. On the negative side, maybe you had issues with certain deliverables which may not have happened if you had not tailored out a process.

85: B

An organization's risk tolerance directly impacts the responses created for risks. A high tolerance means responses may not be too stringent while low tolerance requires very well thought out and tight risk responses.

86: A

There is no value in adding an issue to the lesson learned document without the solution. Similarly, creating a change request document without knowing what the change is useless. Also the work is already pretty much stopped so issuing a notification does not have any value. The best option is to inform the sponsor and affected stakeholders about the issue and that you will provide further details in few days. This is important to avoid surprises to the stakeholders which, if happen, can damage the trust and relationship with the project manager.

87: A

He was referring to the Pareto chart which applies that 80% of the issues are caused by 20% of the factors. So if those 20% factors are modified or corrected, this will resolve 80% of the issues.

88: A

The best approach is to face the speaker and maintain eye contact. This way the team member is not only listening but also taking in non-verbal communication that plays a big role in understanding the message.

89: C

Risk appetite is the degree of uncertainty an organization or an individual is willing to accept for getting a reward. The degree of risk someone will be able to withstand is risk tolerance.

90: B

This is the Initiating process group where stakeholders are identified and recorded on the stakeholder register, business need is identified, and project charter is developed and approved.

91: C

Culture impacts projects, programs and portfolios. The more complex the project the greater the impact of culture is on the project. Culture varies from organization to organization even in the same industry and same geography.

92: A

Project Integration Management is all about coordination and integration of all other project knowledge areas. Thus it describes how processes in different knowledge areas are to interact with each other.

93: C

Project charter template is an organizational process asset and has no link to project or phase closure.

94: A

In Validate Scope process, completed deliverables are submitted to the sponsor for acceptance so either deliverables are accepted or rejected. Rejection may result in a change request. Therefore, accepted deliverables is the correct answer.

95: A

Scope creep can happen whether progressive elaboration is used or not. Actually in a way the chances of scope creep increases in progressive elaboration because the needs, the understanding of the project work, and the efficiency changes during project execution. This can result in scope creep while doing progressive elaboration.

96: C

That process is Develop Project Management Plan where all the plans from various knowledge areas are put together as one integrated plan, though not necessarily as one document.

97: C

Resource leveling is not a solution to this problem. In fact resource leveling may result in extending the schedule for optimizing resource usage.

98: C

Whether it is a non-technology or technology project, the planning process group's objectives are the same. It is to define the project objectives and plan the strategy to meet those objectives. 'Work on the objectives' happens in planning process.

99: C

All this information is found in the communication management plan. The stakeholder register does not discuss communication needs of the stakeholders.

100: A

The fixed price would be the riskiest especially in this case where it is a very large multi-million dollars contract where the scope and specifications of deliverables may not be 100% defined.

101: D

Quality control compares the results of quality measurements with the quality standards set in quality plan while quality assurance audits the quality control measurements and quality plan against the company quality policies and procedures.

102: B

Such a criteria will be described in the administrative closure process documentation/procedure. Close Project or Phase is a process area that includes the administrative closure procedures. Expert judgment is a tool or technique. Project charter is too high level and does not get involved in process level details.

103: A

Templates help in giving a head start and saving time in creating a document. So a template schedule can help in expediting the development of a project schedule.

104: A

This is best handled with a quality assurance audit of the plan and quality control measurements against the company policies. If there is a problem, it could be with the quality plan or the measurements. Quality audit is the right way to uncover that.

105: B

Schedule compression is the technique that is used for reducing the schedule. The schedule can be fast tracked or crashed.

106: B

Configuration management system describes which item can be changed and how, and then what is the process of communicating that change and to whom. Change control board role is only to reject or approve a change. PMIS and project team members are irrelevant here.

107: D

Since they are afraid that you can damage their performance review and impact their bonus, they think you have coercive power.

108: D

Any proposed change requires that it be evaluated before any action can be suggested. Therefore the best option is to ask the customer to send in the details of the scope change in writing so that an evaluation of the proposed change can be done to see how it impacts the project.

109: B

Not all project stakeholders actively support the project. There are always few who have a negative approach or impact on the project and few who take on a very passive role even though project needs their full attention.

110: C

Start-to-Finish relationship is rarely used. This relationship says that once first activity starts then second activity can finish.

111: C

Using six sigma means a maximum of 3.4 defective parts per million is acceptable. Therefore, out of 10,000 it would be zero parts.

112: D

Consultants are not an input to the Direct and Manage Project Work process but these can be a tool and technique (for expert judgment) used in this process.

113: B

By securing data through password protection on both the laptop and the portable backup device you may stop data leak but you will still lose both in the above scenario so this cannot be a response plan for above situation.

114: A

The project manager is using the "good guy, bad guy" technique where he is presenting his boss as the bad guy and himself as good guy to pressure the seller in accepting his terms.

115: B

All scope management plans should include how the scope will be managed and controlled.

116: B

Payments system is a tool and technique of the Control Procurements process and not of the Close Procurements process.

117: B

Cost performance baseline is what is being impacted and will need to be modified once a change request is approved. So cost performance baseline cannot be followed.

Change control board is the one that rejects or approves the change request. There is nothing to follow here.

Monitoring and controlling process group contains all the processes that relate to monitoring and controlling the project. So the process group cannot be followed but a process can be. So this cannot be the choice.

The change's cost estimate has to be followed to implement the change. This estimate will be recommended for approval through the change request and once approved will be used to update the cost performance baseline.

118: C

Mutually exclusive means the events cannot happen at the same time and are totally independent of each other.

119: C

A single program is too big and too vague to be called a feasibility study. A feasibility study may result in a program.

120: A

If the contract has any term that is against the law of the land then such a contract is not legally binding and is unenforceable. Seller unable to perform the work, buyer not making the payments, or contract unacceptable to the legal counsel, does not make the contract invalid.

121: B

The project manager is using the autocratic style where he may or may not be considering expressed opinion of the team members but he is making the decision alone. Also no objection is allowed once the decision has been made. In democratic style, decision would have been made by voting and the majority vote would be the decision.

122: B

Functional manager and portfolio manager will be very much concerned with department's overall strategic goals. Program manager will be more concerned about her role's commitment i.e. program commitments than the department strategic goals. She has invited the three project managers in her program to discuss projects' progress.

123: C

During project execution, actual work is performed for which the plans were developed, deliverables are created, team is managed, etc. So 'Performing the work as per project management plan to achieve project's objectives and goals' is the correct choice.

124: A

To have a valid contract, a deliverable or statement of work must be present; there has to be an offer and acceptance; and buyer's and seller's signatures are required. Seller's contact information is not required for a valid contract.

125: A

First perform impact assessment to understand how this change will affect the project. All other options require that an impact assessment has been done.

126: C

Make active use of progressive elaboration. It means do not spend too much time in detailed planning. Create an overall high level plan, and then plan for the nearest future in detail. As the project progresses, go through detailed planning of next time period. This way you can save time in initiating and planning the project and can move to executing rather quickly. Expert judgment does not speed up the process but it helps in creating an effective result. You cannot move from project charter into executing directly. You need to have a plan.

127: B

Project life cycle does not have any impact on the development of the project charter. This is because charter is to be developed during initiating process of the project while project life cycle is selected during project management planning, which occurs after charter is approved. All other three choices impact the project charter.

128: A

Analogous estimation technique is the best choice when little information is available about the project. The technique uses historical data from similar projects to estimate.

129: D

Identifying business need, dividing project into phases, and evaluating historical information, are all part of project initiation. Project requirements are gathered during the planning process where a requirements document is developed and then the scope statement is created.

130: C

This is the definition of a deliverable. If the template or plan was defined as a deliverable, it can be one of those. Still it is a deliverable.

131: D

Bottom Up estimating technique results in the most accurate estimate, no matter what type of project it is.

132: B

From the scenario, the point of change is the award ceremony and the dinner. The event was supposed to further improve the performance but had the opposite effect. One of the best practices in reward management is to reward the whole team when the whole team is working together to achieve goals. Awarding one or two people can demoralize other team members who now see their fellow team members as competitors. Development of such a feeling destroys the team performance. So the best option is to review the reward system of the project.

133: C

Best option is to see if the schedule can be compressed either by adding more resources and/or fast tracking by running activities in parallel.

134: D

A stakeholder is someone who is impacted by the project or can influence the project so the stakeholder cannot be removed from the project. Discouraging right at the start that very few changes will be entertained will damage the relationship as this message shows that it is more important to reduce number of changes than completing deliverables that give the value expected by the business. Best approach is to involve the stakeholder actively right from the start of the project so that changes get proposed and processed in the early stages when the impact of the change is very low.

135: B

The project budget is the Budget At Completion (BAC) which is $700,000. The rest of the information is not needed to answer this question.

136: A

This is an example of cost of non-conformance which results due to rework, errors, and defects.

137: C

Cost Variance (CV) and Earned Value (EV) are not indices. Cost Planned Index, Schedule Planned Index, Cost Planning Index, and Schedule Performing Index, do not exist. The correct answer is Cost Performance Index (CPI) and Schedule Performance Index (SPI).

138: A

A project charter does not need to be reviewed once approved. If there is significant change in business direction or goals of the project, then it can be reviewed but the purpose is to see if project needs to be cancelled or continued as a new project.

139: C

The business need of the project is included in the project charter and usually is based on the same as in business case. All other choices do not get created until in much later processes.

140: A

Competency can be the issue if significant errors are noted in the work done by a resource. Resource allocation and authority does not have any impact to it. Resource programming is not a term.

141: D

The problem is with deliverables being produced late so there is no need to involve the team leader of the receiving team. Even if second team is still able to produce their deliverables in time, the issue need to be attended to since late deliverables of first team are affecting second team's schedule. The best approach is to discuss with the first team leader why the deliverables are being produced late and what can be done to fix that.

142: A

Reconciling the expense plan with the approved budget happens in the Determine Budget process. The process involves summing up the cost of the project, receiving budget approval, and reconciling approved budget with the expense plan.

143: C

You do not have any power but only influence and impact. So she should classify you as a stakeholder with low influence but high impact.

144: D

Monitor and Control Project Work process considers resource usage data, productivity, budget and schedule variances to assess project performance and predict future performance.

145: B

Statement of work is not a type of contract itself but a component of all types of contracts.

146: B

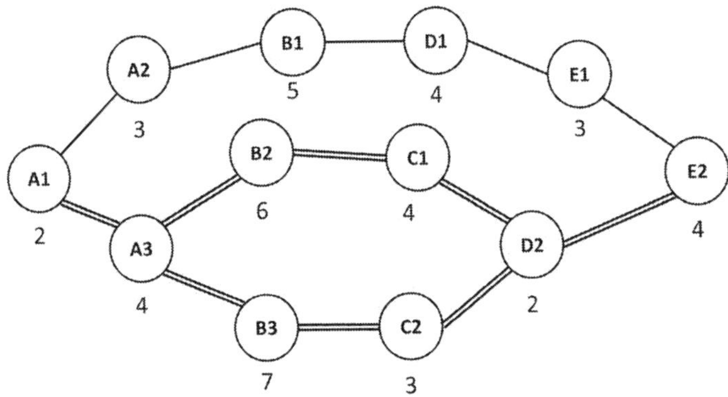

There are two critical paths as shown in diagram with a duration of 22.

147: B

The reason for taking up a project is that there is a business need; therefore it has to be the most important factor to decide which project is selected for implementation. The other three options may be considered as a minor factor but come into play after a project is selected and is being executed.

148: A

Only Develop Project Charter process is in the Initiating Process group. All other processes, mentioned as choices, are part of the Planning process group.

149: A

Safety measures is a characteristic of cost of conformance. All other three are characteristics of cost of nonconformance.

150: D

Contingency reserve and management reserve are not part of the cost performance baseline; therefore planned cost of contingency reserve is not considered when performing earned value analysis.

151: B

Requirements can be managed by using requirements traceability matrix which helps in linking requirements to the project objectives on one side and to the deliverables on the other side.

152: C

Payments to the seller are usually handled by the accounts payable system and not accounts receivable system.

153: B

Although several separate projects for research, getting approval, and marketing would need to be initiated, a coordination and overall control over all these projects is needed. This makes program management as the correct choice. Remember these projects run separately but are highly interrelated.

154: B

Use the integrated change control system to assess if a change to the scope is required and then process that for assessment, review and approval. All other options can only be acted on once an assessment is done and change has been evaluated.

155: A

The seller selection criteria should be reviewed to select the seller for award of the contract. The other three choices can be considered if one or all of these are part of the seller selection criteria.

156: A

Team communication and collaboration becomes more effective when the team is co-located. In terms of communication from project manager, co-location and virtual requires almost same level of communication. Team communication is still required. Cost is dependent on cost of co-location vs. cost of working remotely and cost of communication.

157: A

Any change to the contract requires that the contract change control system be followed. Since the number of resources engaged on the project is written in the contract, any change to it has to follow the contract change control system.

158: B

The warning sign is called a risk trigger which identifies that either a risk has occurred or is imminent.

159: B

It is a formal written communication. It is a project record that can be used for various purposes including creating project progress report.

160: A

When the revenue from improvements becomes equal to the incremental costs to achieve those improvements, optimal quality has been reached. Costs to improve quality further do not increase the revenue at the same rate. This means more money will be spent improving the quality than what will be gained from that improvement.

161: D

She can get a head start by using a WBS from a similar previous project as a template then modify it to fit the new project. It is not a best practice to only drill down 2-3 levels and avoid going to work package detail or completely skip the WBS or ask users to prepare WBS.

162: C

Cost Performance Index (CPI) and Schedule Performance Index (SPI) show the project's progress against the plan. The next logical piece of information should be the forecast to the project completion called as Estimate To Complete (ETC) and Estimate At Completion (EAC).

163: D

Project management plan does not identify the business need of the project plan. The purpose of the plan is to set the course for executing, monitoring and controlling, and closing the project.

164: B

Cost estimate happens farther down after activity definition which follows creation of WBS. Parametric estimate is a tool not an input. Sponsor's commitment does not have any impact on the estimate. Resource breakdown structure is not used in estimation and is irrelevant.

165: A

The total duration of the critical path is,

3+2+3+5+6+12+1+10 = 42 days

Duration of critical path to deployment completion

= 32 days (excludes post deployment support)

Activity 6 which is late by 6 days gets added to the critical path while activity 5 completed 1 day earlier gets deducted from the critical path.

32 + 6 - 1 = 37 days is the minimum time it will take to deploy the project.

166: D

You have to audit seller's invoices so that all required payments can be made to the seller. It is seller's responsibility to take his resources off the project once the work is completed.

167: A

Project budget requirements can be incremental or lump sum. For example, payments may need to be made on a monthly basis. This will be incremental. If the payment is to be made just once, let say, at the end of the project, it will be lump sum. There is the project cost beside contingency and management reserve. Other options are invalid.

168: A

The quality requirements of the project are audited and the results of quality control measurements are reviewed to ensure the requirements are adequate. It also ensures that relevant policies of the organization are followed.

169: A

Project Scope and Procurement Management are not process areas but project management knowledge areas. Close Project or Phase does not include vendor selection. Direct and Manage Project Work process group includes vendor selection and documenting lessons learned.

170: C

Capability Maturity Model Integrated (CMMI) technique is used for performing quality audit of projects.

171: C

All the five process groups must occur at least once in a project life cycle. Without initiation where project charter is developed and approved, project cannot proceed further. Without a plan, there is nothing to execute. Plan describes what to execute. No execution, no monitoring and controlling needed. No closing, project will never end.

172: D

Projects do not need to be always strategic. There are projects that are only executed to keep the lights on and have no other strategic alignment with the organizational strategy.

173: A

The problem is with new surprise issues not with issue management. Same way, poor risk response is not the problem, not having a risk response is. Lip service could be a reason but would be a weak choice. Best choice is that project team is less experienced and is unable to identify, analyze, and response plan all the risks.

174: D

Organizational theory is not considered while developing a project staff management plan. Neither communications strategy nor positions descriptions form part of this plan. Safety is an important aspect when thinking about managing staff and, therefore, is part of the staff management plan.

175: D

Sometimes projects do end without producing a deliverable. A project can be executed just by the project manager alone. Projects may not have a deliverable specified. Project stakeholders can be impacted by the project after it ends. So they may be affected by the project during execution or even after close. This is the correct answer.

176: C

Marginal analysis is the correct choice because it compares benefits and costs of different options and in this case verifies if the gain from improving quality is equal to or lower than the incremental cost to achieve that quality.

177: D

The best option to resolve any dispute with the seller is to go through alternative dispute resolution. These techniques are negotiation, mediation, arbitration, and litigation.

178: A

The customer should use the machine for one year before confirming that all terms of the contract have been met - cannot be a term of final acceptance of the new machine. There could be a support or warranty period defined in the contract that says that for one year the product will be maintained by the manufacturer at no cost to the customer.

179: C

Official approval to proceed with the project work is obtained when the project charter is approved by the sponsor. Stakeholder identification goes on throughout the project life cycle. Deliverable acceptance happens at Validate Scope process which is in monitoring and controlling process group and much later in the project. Project manager usually is assigned at the start of initiating process but it does not mean project is officially being authorized to proceed.

180: B

This is because expected monetary value is not the cost of the risk impact but the probabilistic value of the risk. The project manager being happy with the outcome means that the risk event was expected to be of much higher cost than $15,000 if occurred. There is no indication of being under budget or ahead of schedule in the scenario so these are not correct choices.

181: A

All the 'projects' are in reality operational activity being repeated.

Whether an order is $10 or $300,000 has no bearing on how it is processed. i.e. it is processed the same way. Though each order has a start and end date, there is no unique product, it is the same product. Also no progressive elaboration is to be done.

182: A

Scope management plan provides how the project scope will be managed and controlled. Scope control plan does not exist separately but is included in the scope management plan.

183: C

Influencing is the technique that a project manager uses most often on a project. From initiating to closing, project manager is constantly involved in influencing project stakeholders, sponsor, team members, vendors and functional managers. There is constant negotiation, conflict resolution, and management that requires a highly influential project manager.

184: C

Benchmarking techniques do not measure project performance against the plan. These identify best practices, generate ideas for improvement, and provide a basis for measuring performance.

185: D

Reduction of scope is not part of crashing the schedule or even fast tracking the schedule.

186: B

It is a list of sellers whose qualifications and experiences are found to be competent to perform the work and thus can be invited to bid for the work. Since they are already found to be qualified (pre-qualified) the bid will not include qualification components but only the price, terms and statement of work.

187: B

Work performance data will not be an output of this effort. It was the input that generated this effort.

188: B

In most cases it is impossible to reject a resignation. Distributing the work or fast tracking the schedule both require an assessment of situation already done and course of action decided. So, the best choice is to assess the impact of the lost resource on the project.

189: D

Although it seems that requirement gathering or project planning should be the next step, the first thing to do is to see if all stakeholders are aligned with the project charter and there is no disconnect. This is helpful in two ways, one you validated that the project charter is good to proceed with and second you developed a connection/relationship with all the stakeholders.

190: D

A program is a way to meet business needs by coordinating and controlling multiple related projects. The combined goal of all the projects in a program is the goal of the program. These projects may or may not be running concurrently. It may include a project due to government mandate but others related to market demand as well as several departments could be involved.

191: D

Number of resources, geographical location of resources, and project duration, all have impact on the communication needs of the project. Your experience as a project manager has no bearing on the communication needs of the project.

192: B

Since the project is moving from one phase to another, scope validation should occur in the design phase to validate that all work is completed, then close the phase and initiate the development phase.

193: A

Start the Close Project process, update lessons learned document and perform the administrative closure of the project. It is no different than closing any other type of project.

194: C

It is a less accurate method than bottom-up estimating and is frequently used.

195: B

Rework is an example of internal failure costs. Liabilities is an example of external failure costs. Destructive testing is an example of appraisal costs.

196: C

Enterprise Environmental Factors include project management information system which provides the tools for executing the project. This is the reason these factors are an input to the process. Standard guidelines are organizational process asset. Enterprise environmental factors are not needed in the change request approval process.

197: C

Project team members have the firsthand experience of executing the project, facing issues and solving them, etc. They can provide valuable feedback to be included in lessons learned document.

198: B

Configuration management system is not a part of the change management system but exists separately. It provides the direction of which item needs to be controlled, how it will be changed, if needed, and then specifies who needs to be informed.

199: D

All bidders should be treated equally and fairly. No one should be given preferential treatment because they are first time bidders or have been bidding for long time, have worked on several contracts before, or any other reason. Therefore, the incorrect statement about bidders' conference is that "First time bidders should be given extra attention to encourage them to bid."

200: D

Critical chain method is used when resources are limited because it helps build an effective schedule. It is not called critical path method though a critical path is created when using this method. It creates discretionary dependencies and does not exclusively use mandatory dependencies.

8 - ADDITIONAL PMP MOCK TESTS

This book contains 600 sample PMP questions with answers and explanations. As a special bonus, you can get access to 1,200 more questions by visiting the special offer at http://getxsolution.com/pmp-tests-book-customers/. These have been setup as full length, 200 questions, PMP mock tests of four hours duration each. This means you will have six online simulated tests. You will need the Special Discount Code provided below for this offer to be valid.

Please use the following Special Discount Code: GETXPMPTDISCX

ABOUT THE AUTHOR

Daud Nasir (PMP, LSSBB, Cert. Agile PM, ITIL-Foundation) with over 20 years' experience is an accomplished leader and a seasoned professional in project, program and portfolio management.

Daud has worked with small to large organizations, for example, Hewlett Packard, Procter & Gamble, and General Motors and had excellent exposure to all levels of maturity in the mentioned above domains. This rich experience has helped him to become a highly effective coach and trainer, where he draws examples from various industries, functions, and situations to explain complex concepts. This provides an exceptional learning experience for mentees and trainees.

Daud is a passionate instructor and teaches courses in PMP exam preparation besides several other courses in areas like program management, PMO, business analysis, Lean Six Sigma, and Microsoft Project.

He founded GetXSolution, a Toronto based company with a goal to improve organizational and individual performance through trainings and workshops that truly make a difference in the life of the attendees.

As an active Project Management Institute Volunteer, Daud had the opportunity to contribute to The Guide to the Project Management Body of Knowledge (PMBOK®) 5th Edition as a Subject Matter Expert. Over the years, he has been an evaluator of several awards presented by PMI for excellence in various areas of project management. He also contributed to the Practice Guide for Organizational Project Management.

Connect with Daud now,
LinkedIn: http://ca.linkedin.com/in/daudnasir/
Blog: http://www.DaudNasir.com
Corporate Site: http://www.GetXSolution.com

Made in the USA
Lexington, KY
21 November 2014